I dedicate this book as a small offering
with much love, respect and devotion to

LAMA THUBTEN ZOPA RINPOCHE

My spiritual guide ...
My dearest kind lama
Who grasps all reality
Who has controlled all his senses,
Who takes my heart away
as soon as I lay eyes on him;

When I follow his teaching
and understand his words
and have utmost faith in him
and revere him ...
the good in me begins to flower
and the bad begins to fade ...

I dedicate this book also
to my dearest daughter
JENNIFER TOO

And in accordance with Rinpoche's wish,
I dedicate this book to the ultimate happiness of
all the sentient beings of the world.

May feng shui bring ease to their problems
and bring comfort into their lives

LILLIAN TOO'S
BASIC
FENG SHUI

**AN
ILLUSTRATED
reference manual**

NORTH AMERICAN EDITION

ORIENTAL
PUBLICATIONS

This edition published by:
Oriental Publications
16 Market Street
Adelaide 5000
South Australia
Phone   ~ + 61 8 8212 6055
Fax   ~ + 61 8 8410 0863
E-mail ~oriental@dove.mtx.net.au

National Library of Australia Cataloguing-in Publication:
Bibliography.

ISBN 0 9587113 3 X

Title : Lillian Too's Basic Feng Shui

NORTH AMERICAN EDITION
Published by Oriental Publications
(Under License from Konsep Lagenda Sdn. Bhd.)
Illustrations and Cover Design By Lillian Too
Copyright: © 1997 Lillian Too
Printed by Ritz Print Sdn. Bhd.

North American Edition First published September 1997

meet Lillian Too ...

Lillian Too's credentials speak for
themselves - she was the first woman
in Asia to become the Chief Executive
Officer of a Bank - the Grindlays Dao
Heng Bank in Hong Kong....

In Malaysia where she comes from, Lillian Too is described by Malaysian
Business, the country's leading business magazine as
"... something of a legend in corporate circles being the first woman there
to become the Managing Director of a publicly listed company"

Lillian is an MBA graduate from the Harvard Business School, in Boston
USA; She has also been described as being " in a league of her own "
by one of the country's leading magazines ... SUCCESS magazine. The
internationally acclaimed VOGUE magazine describes her " as someone
people listen to .. "

Lillian was not simply a successful corporate woman. As a business lady
she also made enough money never to have to work again. In the early
Nineties, she retired from working life to become a full time mother.

That was when she started a new career in writing. To date she has
penned fifteen bestsellers, eight of which on her favorite subject of feng
shui, which she says was greatly responsible for giving her masses of luck
during her corporate career days, and in her business dealings ... her feng
shui books have been translated into nine languages.

... her latest achievement has been the phenomenal worldwide success of
her internationally published book THE COMPLETE ILLUSTRATED
GUIDE TO FENG SHUI, published by ELEMENT BOOKS of UK, USA
and Australia which was released in October 1996. This book has made
the bestseller lists of various countries including the UK's Times Book
Watch list The book also recently became the number ONE bestseller in
the BARNES and NOBLE bestseller list of the United States.
Lillian Too is married and has one daughter.

Other books by the author
PUBLISHED BY KONSEP LAGENDA SDN BHD
Feng Shui
Applied Pa Kua Lo Shu Feng Shui
Practical Applications of Feng Shui
Chinese Numerology in Feng Shui
Water Feng Shui for Wealth
Dragon Magic - my feng shui stories
Chinese Astrology for Romance and Relationships
The Chinese Dragon
Strategies for Career Success
Creative Visualization
Tap the Power Inside You
Explore the Frontiers of your Mind

PUBLISHED BY ELEMENT BOOKS U.K, Australia and USA
The Complete Illustrated Guide to Feng Shui.

PUBLISHED BY BERITA PUBLISHERS
Making your First Million

ALL TRADE ENQUIRIES TO

In UK and Europe
MILLBANK BOOKS
The Courtyard,
Windhill, Bishops Stortford
Hertsfordshire
CM 23 2PE, United Kingdom
Tel: 1279 655 233
Fax: 1279 655 244
Email: millbank@demon.co.uk

In Australia & New Zealand
ORIENTAL PUBLICATIONS
16 Market Street,
Adelaide 5000,
South Australia

Tel: 61 8 8212 6055
Fax: 61 8 8410 0863
Email: oriental @dove.mtx.net.au

LILLIAN TOO'S BASIC FENG SHUI contents:

LILLIAN
TOO'S
BASIC
FENG SHUI
<u>contents:</u>

LILLIAN
TOO'S
BASIC
FENG SHUI
contents:

7 KITCHENS, TOILETS, STORE ROOMS, STAIRCASES & CEILINGS pages 157 to 167

8 ENHANCING THE LIVING SPACE pages 168 to 180

LILLIAN
TOO'S
BASIC
FENG SHUI
<u>contents:</u>

9 USING
FORMULA FENG SHUI   pages 181 to 191

A BLESSING FROM
MY PRECIOUS GURU   page 190

Lillian Too is something of a legend in Malaysian corporate circles .. with a formidable c.v. ... **MALAYSIAN BUSINESS**

The pursuit of excellence is one never ending story for Lillian Too. Having reached the peak of the corporate world years ago, she has now turned her sights onto new things ... like writing ...
SUCCESS MAGAZINE

Too is a person who practices what she preaches ...
NEW STRAITS TIMES

In an arena largely dominated by men, Too stood out like a rose among the thorns ...but this rose knew what she was doing, and did it better than most of her male counterparts .... **THE SUN - BUSINESS PAGE**

Everything around her ... is reflective of her warm, vibrant personality ... and though she considers herself retired, to the readers of her best-selling books throughout Malaysia, she's only just begun ...
BUSINESS TIMES

Too's credentials are impeccable .... **SARAWAK SUNDAY TRIBUNE**

All good things come to those who wait ... after climbing the corporate career ladder for two decades, ... now, retired ... Lillian Too is getting the kind of attention most people only dream of **... STAR**

Anyone suffering from a crisis of confidence could do well to spend some time in the company of the very spirited Lillian Too ... **LEADER**

Lillian Too's talk ... was as breathtaking as the person herself ...
MALAYSIAN INDUSTRY

She is introduced as a lady of many seasons, one with many accomplishments, constantly pursuing new frontiers and always meeting up with success ... **CERTIFIED MANAGEMENT DIGEST**

Lillian Too, the woman with the Midas touch .... has made her mark as a professional businesswoman ... **CORPORATE WORLD**

風水

THE SCIENCE OF FENG SHUI WITH LILLIAN TOO

The Secrets of Chinese wisdom for
Health, Wealth and happiness, simply explained

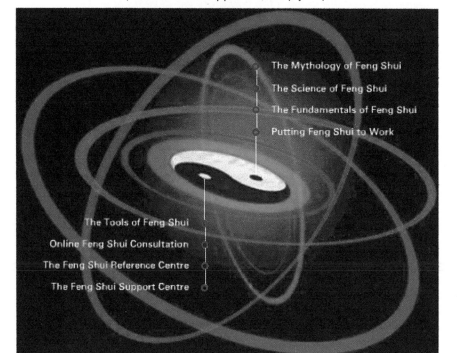

The Mythology of Feng Shui

The Science of Feng Shui

The Fundamentals of Feng Shui

Putting Feng Shui to Work

The Tools of Feng Shui

Online Feng Shui Consultation

The Feng Shui Reference Centre

The Feng Shui Support Centre

meet Lillian Too on INTERNET

http://www.asiaconnect.com.my/lillian-too

http://www.dragonmagic.com

EMAIL

ltoo@popmail.asiaconnect.com.my

1 INTRODUCTION

Feng shui is an ancient science that has its roots in the Chinese way of viewing the Universe, where all things on Earth are categorized into five basic elements, and take on implications of positive or negative energy. This is termed *chi,* and it can have either *yin* or *yang* attributes.

Feng shui, is literally translated to mean *wind* and *water.* It is the science of selecting a living environment where the elements and the energies are in harmonious balance, thereby bringing the good life to those who reside within that environment.

Feng shui is also an art - a skill borne of experience and common sense - the skill of arranging one's immediate living and work space to further strengthen this vital balance and harmony.

A certain amount of mysticism surrounds the practice of feng shui. Understanding its many precepts requires the acceptance of fundamental theories about the Universe which may seem alien in the context of modern day perceptions of the way the world works. Descriptions of landscapes and environments are shrouded in symbolic representations. And metaphors that embrace classical and mythical Chinese references to animals, elements and the intangible forces of yin and yang energies reflect the ancient roots of this science.

The theory of feng shui may be studied by going to source books that have survived, but the practical applications of feng shui journeyed down the centuries by word of mouth, passed on from generation to generation - thereby giving it connotations of superstition. Thus while the philosophy of feng shui is simple, and the promise of feng shui is meaningful abundance, prosperity and happiness, its practice in a modern context requires an understanding of its fundamentals, access to its various formulas, and sufficient experience that allow for meaningful and correct interpretations of its guidelines and practice.

The Chinese people have always believed in feng shui, except to those whose knowledge of, and exposure to it is limited, feng shui is usually practiced as superstition. In **ancient China**, only the privileged classes had access to feng shui knowledge. Feng shui was the exclusive domain of the Imperial family and the mandarins who enjoyed the emperors' patronage. There are even tales of how emperors would go out of their way to obscure the old texts, thereby preventing those who might be a threat to the dynasty from practicing feng shui . The first Ming emperor, it was speculated, decreed that the kingdom be flooded with books that contained misleading theories and wrong guidelines on feng shui. Centuries later, when Mao Tze Tung became the new emperor of China, he too believed in feng shui. Mao was obsessed by the fall of previous emperors and spent a lifetime studying the Twenty Four Annals of the Dynasties, and throughout his reign, Mao banned the practice of feng shui in China.

feng shui crosses the great waters

Even as feng shui waned in China, Chinese who had fled the motherland and settled in faraway countries continued to keep the practice alive. Feng shui flourished in **Taiwan.** When Chiang Kai Shek fled the mainland, he took with him thousands of old texts on feng shui. Many feng shui Masters also went with Chiang, and they continued to put their skills to work - in the process, benefiting the feng shui of Chiang's regime, as well as the island's business community. It is surely not a coincidence that Taiwan is so prosperous today !

Feng shui also continued to flourish in **Hong Kong**, where many Chinese refugees settled. Today, Hong Kong has become the unofficial capital of feng shui, and Chinese residents here consider feng shui a way of life. Even the first post 1997 Chinese Governor of Hong Kong - CH Tung - has indicated he will not move into either the colonial Governor's mansion nor the colonial Governor's old office because he believes both locations suffer from inauspicious feng shui ! Like the true Chinese he is, his new office will be checked by the feng shui master to ensure luck is on his side in the difficult days ahead …

Probably the most exciting development of recent years has been the re appearance of feng shui in China. The practice has been brought back by overseas Chinese now investing in business ventures in the new China. Whole townships and property projects spearheaded by Hong Kong Chinese for instance, now reveal evidence of the feng shui man's inputs !

Unlike the old days, books on feng shui are today easily available, and with some effort, anyone can practice feng shui ...

Another exciting development has been the growing acceptance and popularity of feng shui amongst Western educated Chinese now living in the Chinatowns of the United States, Canada, Australia, UK, Europe and South East Asia. In places where there are significant pockets of an overseas Chinese population - like Singapore and Malaysia, feng shui continues to grow in popularity. Many are eagerly rediscovering the wonderful promise of a practice that is part of their cultural heritage.

And in tandem with this growing acceptance of feng shui amongst overseas Chinese has been another equally exciting phenomena, the increasing awareness of, and acceptance accorded to, feng shui by the other communities of the world.

all over the world people are discovering the great promise of feng shui

Feng shui in the West started as part of the New Age movement that focused on the totality of the mind, body and spirit of mankind.

New Age sought out the esoteric teachings of the East, and in the process discovered the great promise and potential of feng shui. In recent years feng shui has gone beyond New Age and is now enjoying growing mainstream appeal ... thus has feng shui crossed the great waters to all corners of the globe. Today this wonderful science is accessible to everyone, and those who practice it have discovered that living in harmony with their personal environments can indeed bring great abundance, wonderful opportunities, good health, personal happiness and even serious wealth and prosperity into their lives.

the philosophy of tien, ti ren

While feng shui promises much in terms of bringing material and physical well being to those who arrange their living and work environments according to its precepts, it is not magic.

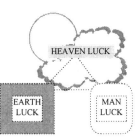

Feng shui is not a spiritual practice which create miracles. It does not bring overnight success. It does not change a person's life situation immediately.

Tien, Ti, Ren
represents the trinity of luck that governs our material well being. Feng shui is Ti, the luck from the earth

Feng shui works according to the quality of the energies that surround any living or work space. Those who would promise instant wealth, striking the lottery and creating immediate gratification do not truly understand the philosophy of feng shui.

Feng shui cannot create overall good fortune on its own. What it can do is create favorable energy around your home and your office so that when bad luck strikes, it tempers the ill fortune and reduces the loss, making things easier to bear. And when one is going through a time of good fortune according to one's fate or destiny, then beneficial feng shui enhances the good fortune - bringing greater good luck than if there had been bad feng shui.

This is based on the philosophy of *tien, ti and ren* - the Chinese words for heaven, earth and mankind. This is the trinity of luck.

There is **heaven luck** which one is born with.
Heaven luck or *tien chai* is <u>not</u> within any one's control. No one has dominion over the circumstances of his or her birth, nor of the good and bad periods of one's life. This is why all the great cultures of the world have divination methods that attempt to read one's fate and destiny based on birth charts and other methods of fortune telling. This is why prayer is so powerful, and why religion is such a vital part of life's existence.
Divine help from heaven is not under mankind's control and it is not to be confused with feng shui.

But **earth luck**, *ti chai* is within our control. Earth luck is the luck that comes from the environment and this gets strengthened when the feng shui of one's surroundings is auspicious.

Viewed within this context , feng shui takes on significant perspective, for if earth luck is within one's control - and indeed, we can actively create good feng shui in our homes and offices - then positively doing something to improve our personal environments must surely and significantly illuminate our life's luck. Feng shui becomes then a vital component of the circumstances of one's being, for it addresses that part of our destiny over which we can exercise control.

complement good earth luck with equally worthy mankind luck

Feng shui luck brings opportunities, improves chances of success, enhances our living condition and creates peace and goodwill in our relationships.

But feng shui luck reaches its <u>maximum</u> potential only when accompanied by equally strong and excellent **mankind luck** - *ren chai* - and this, as the name suggests, is also within our control.

Thus while having good feng shui brings opportunities for advancement and the promise of higher incomes, if one does not seize the opportunity, or work at complementing one's propitious fortune with good old fashioned hard work, a positive attitude and a determined outlook, all of which are components of mankind luck, then all your good feng shui gets squandered ! Mankind luck is the luck you create for yourself !

How can anyone who does not take his work seriously enjoy good feng shui in his work ? Feng shui is only one third of the overall luck that determines how successful you can be. When added to the luck you create for yourself however, feng shui luck becomes a truly formidable ally.

Feng shui practice can be applied to almost every facet of the living and working condition. It has to do with enhancing the energies of the surrounding environment as well as the immediate living and work space. It functions on the premise that if one lives - breathes, sleeps, sits, eats, and works - surrounded by healthy vibrant energy, then one will be enveloped by an aura of good vibrations that attract excellent good fortune. On the other hand if one is shrouded by bad energy, dead energy, killing energy ... then the environment brings grave misfortunes.

Good luck comes in a variety of different ways, and encompass all the physical, mental and spiritual aspirations of mankind. Bad luck also comes in different guises and run the gamut from ill health to loss to missing opportunities, to being plagued by injury, failure and betrayal. Enjoying good feng shui gives you a very serious edge over your competitors. Suffering from bad feng shui places you at an acute disadvantage. Feng shui principles should be put to use in your home and in your place of work. If you are in business, it should be

apply feng shui to your home and to your place of work

applied to your office, your retail and branch outlets, your factories, and your warehouses. If you are a career person, feng shui should be activated at your desk, and each time you undertake an important assignment.

Your home can be a luxury mansion, or a modest cottage. Feng shui can be applied irrespective of how grand or humble your home may be.

Your home can be a bungalow, a town house, an apartment, or a single room, shared with someone or at college. Your home can be rented or owned. It can be temporary or permanent. Any space where you retire to at the end of each day for rest, relaxation and rejuvenation should offer you the benefits of an auspicious and harmonious flow of energy. When your home enjoys good feng shui, you will be wrapped with vibrant and revitalizing energy.

Each of the rooms in your home can benefit from feng shui -the public areas like living rooms and the dining rooms, as well as the private areas like family and bed rooms. Layout, orientations, shapes, color schemes, placement of furniture, decorative objects and paintings - all add to the totality of the whole. How to put them all together to directly benefit the residents is what feng shui application is about.

applying feng shui comes with practice

The best way to go about it is to take a systematic approach, and this book lays out the steps from chapter to chapter. In so doing, it is necessary to first understand at least the basic fundamentals and concepts of feng shui.

 **learn to see with feng shui eyes**

Practice feng shui awareness and develop a solutions oriented attitude. Remember that there are practical and inexpensive remedies to most feng shui problems, and it is seldom necessary to resort to drastic expensive measures.

One can apply a combination of the various schools of feng shui. Do not be surprised by the multitude of feng shui guidelines that seem to proliferate in the market place today. Different masters may offer different recommendations depending on where and how they acquired their knowledge. Remember that amongst the old masters who live in the East, few would willingly divulge what they rightly regard as their *trade secrets*. And even amongst the Chinese, different dialect groups take different approaches to the practice.

When in doubt go back to basics, and apply a healthy dose of common sense. Do not confuse the set of guidelines that apply to the Form school with those associated with the Compass school. The approach adopted by both are completely divergent. Nevertheless, neither schools can be ignored, and both depend on the fundamental concepts for interpretations.

with practice You can do Your own feng shui

So focus on developing a working knowledge of the fundamental concepts. With practice you can do your own feng shui.

In the old days, feng shui enjoyed immense royal patronage. Emperors were particularly concerned about the orientation of imperial burial grounds. The view was held that the fortunes of the living were largely determined by the quality of ancestral feng shui, and China is full of legends and village tales that describe in lyrical terms, the graves of the fathers of founding emperors like Chu Yuan Chuan, who founded the Ming dynasty, or of Sun Yat Sen, the man who became the president of China around the turn of the century. Visitors to Beijing can, if they wish, motor to the Northern outskirts of the city to view the Ming tombs which were constructed according to strict feng shui guidelines.

feng shui in ancestral burial grounds

In more recent times it has also been speculated that both Mao Tze Tung and Deng Xiao Ping owed their rise to power to the most special orientation of their respective ancestors' graves.

Designing ancestral graves according to feng shui is a practice that is still popular in Taiwan where wealthy families go to great lengths not only to bury their dead in an auspicious orientation, but also ensure that grave sites are properly maintained and guarded. In particular, they make certain that the drainage and water flows are always auspicious. Living patriarchs of prominent families also select their burial plot in advance to ensure that family fortunes stay intact, and that descendants continue to bring honor to the family name. This practice is also discreetly followed by the rich Chinese of Singapore, Malaysia and Indonesia.

and in the planning of towns & cities

In times past, feng shui also featured strongly in the planning of towns & cities. Canton's prosperity was due to its propitious location on the Pearl river delta, while Shanghai's famous bund was believed to have brought great wealth to this metropolis. Hong Kong itself at the start of the century was no more than a barren rock, but with proper feng shui observance by the local population, and aided by the excellent orientations of its harbor the colony has continued to prosper.

The practice of feng shui in today's world differs substantially from its historical perspectives. To start with, feng shui today is freely available to everyone. Feng shui is used by rich and poor alike, as a result of which the practice is applied to individual residences and work places, and by individuals.

Secondly feng shui today is being practiced in a world that is far different from that of its origins.

Because the physical landscape of the world has changed so much, the practice of feng shui today represents a great deal of adaptation of old precepts.

The growth of cities and the popularity of apartment living in an urban setting has caused a certain amount of re interpretation of the old texts. New meanings have thus been attributed to old metaphors.

applying feng shui to today's world requires new interpretation of old texts

Thus dragons and tigers, turtles and phoenixes are superimposed onto a cityscape for purposes of interpreting landscape and form school feng shui in a modern metropolis.

In a modern city of high rises, man made buildings such as this have come to be regarded as *mountains* .. and depending on shapes, location and structure, they are likened to the celestial animals of landscape feng shui.

Highways have been described as rivers while city roads become purveyors of *chi* flows. Skyscrapers and large buildings are now regarded as mountains and elevated landforms, and so become symbolic of one of the celestial creatures - with their shapes determining what kind of element they are categorized as.

Making this leap in interpretation requires careful application of the theories that make up the basis and the historical context of feng shui applications. Once again therefore, it becomes necessary to refer back to the underlying fundamental concepts upon which all the schools of feng shui , and all its compass formulas are based. It is necessary to always bear this in mind.

yin dwellings of the dead

In the old days, feng shui was extensively applied to *yin* dwellings, basically ancestral burial grounds. The textbooks on feng shui treat *yin* feng shui as a subject that is separate and different from *yang* feng shui. Symbols and reference points for the purposes of calculations differ for these two types of dwellings.

The feng shui that is referred to in all my books is *yang* feng shui and are applicable only to *yang* dwellings - or houses of the living. This is not to say that *yin* feng shui is no longer practiced today. In Taiwan it remains a very important dimension of the feng shui that is practiced by many of its prominent families. Ancestral burial grounds for the older generation of families, are usually purchased long before their demise, with the grave of the family patriarch receiving the most careful attention. This is because the fortunes of the descendants is said to be substantially affected by the feng shui of the immediate ancestor's grave.

Backed by mountain

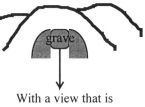

In Malaysia, *yin* feng shui continues to be studied and practiced by a small group of enthusiastic practitioners, and some of the more prominent patriarchs of wealthy business families have already selected their graves, and had them designed according to basic landscape feng shui, ie with the grave backed by a mountain and facing a view that is not blocked ... as shown here.

With a view that is not blocked

Yin feng shui is said to particularly affect the male descendants of the family. Female descendants are less affected by ancestral burial grounds. Nevertheless, because one has little control over the actual orientation of most graves in a modern cemetery, I have always advocated that to be on the safe side, it might be better not to have a grave at all for one's ancestor. Especially since the alternative - cremation - is both respectable and acceptable. According to feng shui experts, the effect on descendants luck is totally neutral - neither good nor bad, when the patriarch is cremated. This approach allows us peace of mind when we are forced to decide how we should bury our dead. This also puts the focus squarely on *yang* dwellings, which is far more meaningful, and easy to do.

yang dwellings of the living

All of the feng shui guidelines and tips contained in this book pertain to *yang* dwellings or houses of the living. This distinction is important to note since the basic tool used in all the recommendations given are based on the *Later Heaven* arrangement of trigrams in the *Pa Kua* which differs substantially from the *Early Heaven* arrangement of trigrams. Please see a later section in chapter 3 for a more detailed explanation of the arrangement of the trigrams in the Pa Kua.

A second reason for making this distinction is to draw the reader's attention to the intrinsic difference between *yin* and *yang* energies. Houses of the living are deemed to be yang because yang energy represents life, activity, movement and growth. Yin energy on the other hand, suggests stillness, silence, and death. When applying feng shui to yang dwellings therefore, it is vital to understand that yang influences should dominate, though never to the extent that yin energies are completely absent. Please see the section on yin and yang in chapter 2 for a thorough explanation.

Understanding the difference between yin and yang feng shui enables the amateur practitioner to understand why the experts always recommend against siting one's home within the vicinity of buildings that have yin dominated energies. Places like hospitals, prisons, cemeteries, abattoirs, slaughter houses and so forth generate too much yin energy, which creates the kind of vibrations that are entirely unsuitable for yang dwellings. They are thus to be avoided.

> avoid living too near to hospitals cemeteries, and prisons ...the yin energy is too strong

Experts also warn against living in buildings built on land which previously housed these places, since the yin energies there previously, are believed to continue to linger. Hence when looking for a suitable new home, it is always a good idea to investigate the recent history of the site upon which your new home will be located. Avoid locations where death or killing at some time in the recent past was a regular occurrence.

If you already live near yin energy dominated places and absolutely cannot move out, the feng shui remedy is to introduce features which create yang energies that effectively balance out the yin energies. If you live too near a cèmetery, paint the side of the wall that faces the cemetery a bright red ! This will absorb the yin energy emanating from the cemetery.

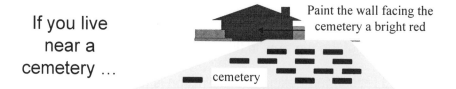

If you live near a cemetery ...

Paint the wall facing the cemetery a bright red

cemetery

If you live next to a hospital, a nursing home, a police station or even a prison, a very effective way to counter the yin energy is to erect two tall and bright spotlights between your house and the building. If you live in an apartment next to a hospital place a bright light in any of the windows that open to a view of the hospital or other such structure.

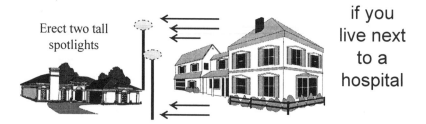

Erect two tall spotlights

if you live next to a hospital

If you live in a home that is built on land which was previously a cemetery, or had a hospital or any other yin dominated structure on it, paint your walls a bright color, keep the radio on for the best part of the day, and create activity within your home. If your home is left empty for most part of the day when you are at work and the kids are at school, keep the radio or TV turned on, OR keep a pet - a dog or a cat - this is the best way of activating valuable yang energy.

Even if your home does not suffer from the affliction dealt with here, implementing all of the suggestions above will be auspicious as it represents good feng shui to generate yang energies.

some preliminary questions answered

Question: Does feng shui always work ?
Answer: Yes. If you get it right, feng shui always improves your living and work condition. But feng shui is not a magic cure all for every one of your problems. Remember that feng shui represents only one third of the trinity of luck. If you are not fated to become a big tycoon, feng shui may make you rich, but not seriously wealthy ! That depends on your *heaven luck*. And if your home enjoys good feng shui you will find yourself becoming more busy. You will be presented with opportunities to enhance your life or improve your income. You must create your own *mankind luck* by seizing these opportunities, and accepting your good fortune.

Question: How do I know if I my home has bad feng shui ?
Answer: You know something is wrong if you suffer a series of unfortunate occurrences shortly after moving into a new home e.g. if your family take turns getting sick, or you losing your job for no good reason, or getting involved in an accident, or getting robbed ... bad luck can sometimes be due to your own astrological chart seeing you through a bad period but if every person living in the same home seems to be suffering from bad luck, perhaps it might be useful to check whether something harmful is affecting the feng shui of your home.

Question: What if my bad luck is due to the bad feng shui of my father's grave - is there anything I can do to correct it ?
Answer: I am not an expert on yin feng shui so I cannot help you, but yes, you can correct the feng shui of your ancestor's grave if you suspect something is wrong. People in Taiwan do it all the time. But you must be careful. Yin feng shui is very powerful - you could make things worse, and you will also be affecting the feng shui of your brothers and sisters. So you should get their consent if you plan to make any changes. My advice is to look for a feng shui master who is an expert on yin feng shui. My *si fu,* Mr. Yap Cheng Hai is very knowledgeable. He might be able to help, if he can be persuaded to take on such an onerous project.

2 NINE BASIC CONCEPTS

 The practice of feng shui always starts with the first conceptual principle. This is the importance of location. If the whereabouts of your home is auspicious according to basic feng shui tenets, this alone will assure you and your family of a good life. Excellent luck will accompany you and all your endeavors as long as you live in such a home. The natural environment is extremely powerful, and even if your interiors might suffer from feng shui mistakes, the effect will be insignificant if the location of your home enjoys excellent classical form school feng shui.

Landscape feng shui focuses initially on the physical surroundings of your home. If you live in an apartment, use the whole building in which your apartment is situated to determine if your location follows good feng shui landscape criteria..

The best location according to classical feng shui is pictorially represented here. This is defined in lyrical animal metaphors that refer to elevated landforms.
These are the four celestial animals of classical feng shui.

The **black turtle hills** are the mountains behind, which are ideally to be placed in the North direction.

Turtle hills

Tiger hills

Ideal home location

Dragon hills

Phoenix foot stool

The **green dragon hills** are on the left, and ideally should be in the East.
The **white tiger hills** are on the right which should ideally be in the West, and these hills must be lower than the dragon hills on the left and the turtle hills behind. And finally there is the **red phoenix hillock** in front, ideally placed South, with a river hugging the site like a jade belt !
The overall shape resembles an *armchair* symbolizing a life of comfort.

This configuration is so auspicious, rich Chinese tycoons in the Far East countries actually have this contour of landforms artificially created around their family mansion to ensure they enjoy excellent feng shui. And it works !

Although in the old days feng shui experts went to great trouble to look for exactly this configuration, in today's world where auspicious natural landscapes can be artificially simulated and constructed it is being done with great success ! **How ?**

the cardinal rule is … mountain behind water in front

By following the cardinal rule of feng shui and that is to have the mountain behind, and water in front ! Contours of the landscape are very significant in feng shui, and undulating landscapes are always preferred to those that are totally flat . But the most vital rule to follow is never to have the mountain in front blocking your main door. The area in front of your home, and your front door should be left empty. The view must not be blocked. And if there is a water flow ie a river flowing in front, in full view of the home, then the feng shui is extremely auspicious !

In modern landscapes, this cardinal rule of feng shui indicates that if there is any tall or large building near where you live, make sure it is behind your home, not in front ! Thus:

This tall building situated behind this small cottage is excellent for the cottage as it simulates the black turtle hills that is supposed to be behind.

Meanwhile, the land on the left of this house (inside looking out) should be slightly higher than land on the right. This simulates the green dragon and white tiger hills. If it is the other way round, the effect is inauspicious because it means the tiger dominates the dragon and can then turn against the residents.

If there is empty land or a view of water in front, the feng shui of this cottage is vastly improved

The celestial animals - the turtle the dragon, the tiger, and the phoenix are important and powerful symbols of landscape feng shui. Appreciating their significance enables the amateur practitioner to correct and enhance their home locations.

NORTH

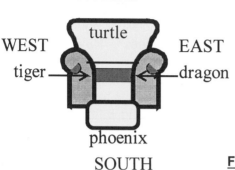

WEST

EAST

tiger

dragon

phoenix

SOUTH

The *armchair* formation is not easy to find in the natural landscape, nor is it within everyone's budget, but it can be ingeniously simulated. This is how it can be done.

The celestial animals can also be activated to bring good luck into the home.

First take care of your back ! The ground behind should be higher than the land in front, so if you can, create a little mound that resembles the back of the turtle. Your home will then enjoy feng shui protection. Ideally the place of the turtle should represent the NORTH sector of your home, but if this is not possible, it does not matter ...

The turtle symbolizes support from important people, long life ... and protection

If you absolutely cannot create higher ground behind, hang a painting or picture of a turtle in the back portion of your home, or better still keep a turtle, or any of its relatives - the tortoise or terrapin in the back part of your home. Or in the NORTH part of your home. It is not necessary to go overboard. Keep one, NOT a whole family ! The number associated with the turtle is the number 1. If you cannot keep a real turtle, a ceramic or bronze one will do just fine.

Activating the turtle in the home is one of the best feng shui features to have ...

16

The dragon is the ultimate good luck symbol. This mythical creature has a very special place in the hearts and minds of the Chinese people.

In landscape feng shui, physical landforms that can house the green dragon are the best indication that a site is auspicious. Indeed, much of authentic feng shui practice involves searching for exactly hills and mountains where this celestial creature exists.

Only undulating land can house dragons !

Look for land that is undulating rather than flat, where the grass grows verdant and green, where the soil is fertile, where the air smells good and where the site is relatively sheltered from strong winds. Avoid mountain tops that are exposed to the elements, and land where even the grass cannot grow. Let there be the presence of both sunlight and shade so that yin blends harmoniously with yang

natural landscape

Let the dragon hills be on the left side of your home by ensuring that land on your left is higher than land on your right

Turtle hills behind

house

Let the neighbor on your left be slightly higher than the neighbor on your right. If you live in an apartment, apply the same principle to buildings to the left and right of you.

urban landscape

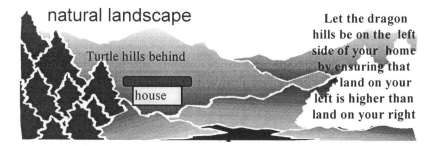

right ← → left

When looking for a place with good feng shui, be particularly alert to the contours of the surroundings. When the road is sloping, sites that are halfway between the highest and lowest point are better than being right at the top or at the bottom. Being at the top of a hill is said to be inauspicious since there is little protection from the elements. Being in the valley is less problematic than being at the top, but mid levels is where you want to be !

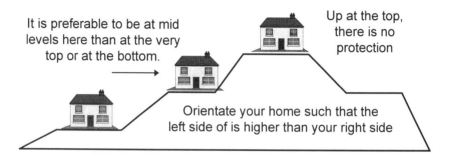

It is preferable to be at mid levels here than at the very top or at the bottom.

Up at the top, there is no protection

Orientate your home such that the left side of is higher than your right side

Try not to live below road level

If your land is below road level, build at least a two level house, and let the upper level be higher than the road.

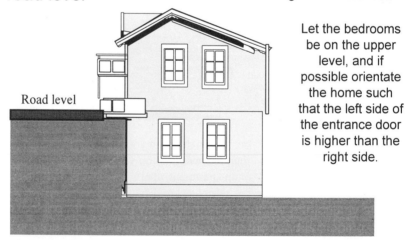

Road level

Let the bedrooms be on the upper level, and if possible orientate the home such that the left side of the entrance door is higher than the right side.

Do not let the house stand on exposed stilts since this creates empty space beneath the house which symbolizes a lack of foundation. Always close up the lower levels and place proper rooms there. Let the house *hug* the hillside, much like a *dragon's lair*. This transforms a potentially inauspicious home into a very auspicious home.

you can also activate the Dragon inside your home The green dragon is said to reside in the East ... if you live in an apartment and have little control over the larger landscape considerations, it is an excellent idea to activate the dragon within your home by placing either a painting of a dragon on any of the East walls of your home, OR place a ceramic representation of the dragon on the East side of your living room.

The dragon is the most popular good fortune symbol used by the Chinese, especially by those in business. If you plan on using the dragon, do not use a dragon with five claws since this is the imperial dragon, and the *yang* energies which it symbolizes may be too strong for you. Go for the normal four clawed dragon. For the same reason, also make sure that the dragon you use as a decorative object is not too large.

If you use the dragon as a corporate logo, do not imprison the dragon inside a circle or square, and make sure it looks fat, happy and prosperous. One of the best examples of the effective use of the dragon as a corporate logo is the Hong Leong Group of Malaysia. Their dragon is not only fat, it also looks pregnant, suggesting plenty of offsprings, or successful acquisitions for the Group.

Do not place any representation of the dragon inside the bedroom. The dragon is the ultimate yang symbol and is not suitable for a place of rest where yin energies are far more important.

It is also useful to note that for some people placing the dragon inside the home may cause residents to become too aggressive. If you feel yourself becoming too energetic after placing this creature in your home, it is advisable not to use this method of energizing your home. On the other hand if you experience new opportunities and better luck, then you have an affinity with this creature, and you would do well to continue.

The <u>white tiger</u> is as important as the green
dragon and is always found where there is the *true* dragon.
Please remember that in feng shui language references to these
celestial animals always refer to hills and landforms. Thus if
dragon hills are present, then it can be assumed that tiger hills are
also present.

**Tiger hills
must always
be lower
than
Dragon hills**

The art of landscape feng shui is in determining
which are the dragon hills and which the tiger hills.
This is not as difficult as it sounds. Usually the hills
on the east of your home are said to be dragon hills
and hills on the west are said to be tiger hills. An
alternative method of determining the difference is
that the hills to the left of your front door are dragon
hills and hills to your right are tiger hills.

The proviso is that the higher hills must represent the dragon !
If the higher hills are on your right, or on the west side of your home, then the
orientation is said to be <u>inauspicious</u> ! This is because the tiger is said to have
become dominant and more powerful than the dragon - an extremely dangerous
configuration because then there is the danger that the tiger could
turn against the residents of the home.
**Meanwhile please note that while references are made to <u>hills</u> here, the
principle is equally applicable to any <u>land</u> to the left and right of your home.**

The most auspicious spot
is where the dragon hills meet with
the tiger hills

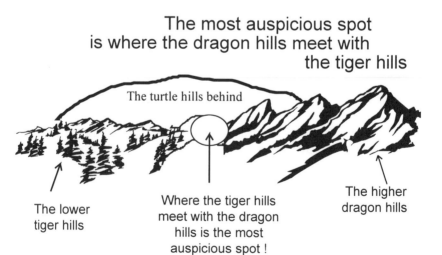

The turtle hills behind

The lower
tiger hills

Where the tiger hills
meet with the dragon
hills is the most
auspicious spot !

The higher
dragon hills

The <u>crimson phoenix</u> symbolizes the South, or the area that lies in front of your residence. This part of the configuration should be flat, or at least lower than the back, the left or the right of the home, and the view should be unencumbered.

The phoenix is said to represent opportunities that bring material comforts. If the front of your home is blocked by any structure, mountain or hill, the result could well be that everything you undertake will get blocked. Success is hard to come by, and worse, you could suffer severe losses. In short the feng shui is most inauspicious.

The crimson phoenix is represented by a small hillock that is said to represent the footstool for you to rest your weary legs. Especially for a home, the presence of this hillock is most auspicious since it allows residents to relax and gather their energies to face the world outside their homes.

The view in front of the house, especially directly ahead of the main door should not be blocked by any structure or hill for at least twice the length of the home.

It is possible to *symbolically* activate the phoenix by placing a decorative <u>bird</u> in the south

A small elevation, or even a rock on the front lawn to represent the phoenix is an auspicious feature.

I have a pink marble flamingo in the South corner of my garden, which brings me lots of opportunities …

I also have a stunning painting of a Rooster on the South side of my living room

21

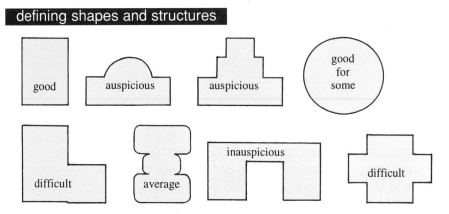

The shapes and structures of everything in the physical landscape are a big part of feng shui. The conceptual principles behind the meanings of shapes - and whether they are auspicious or inauspicious - are diagnosed according to:

- whether the shapes are regular or irregular
- whether there are missing corners
- whether there are protruding corners
- the *element* attribute of the shape itself
- whether the shape resembles a lucky or unlucky symbol

auspicious shapes

Regular shapes are always luckier than irregular shapes

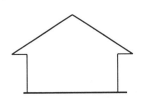

Any shape that is a perfect square or rectangular, whether flat, to represent the layout shape of rooms, or standing to represent the vertical shape of buildings or furniture is always regarded as auspicious. This is considered to be the most regular shape and is highly recommended because it is easy to enhance the feng shui of buildings constructed in such shapes.

The shape shown here is the typical shape of a standard house. Notice it has a rectangular body and a roof which narrows to a point upwards. The silhouetted effect shows an upward pointing arrow - indicating movement upwards and growth. It is thus a very auspicious shape.

Irregular shapes give rise to missing corners

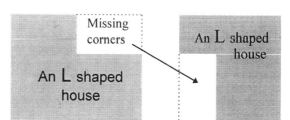

Missing corners always create problems in Interior feng shui, and the severity of the problem depends on which corner is missing. Thus if you divide your home layout into nine equal grids and check the compass direction of each of the grids you will be able to identify the compass direction of the corner that is missing. The way to divide the home into the nine sector grid is shown here.

An L shaped house

The missing corner in this example of an L shaped house is the NE corner according to the compass reading shown here.

N

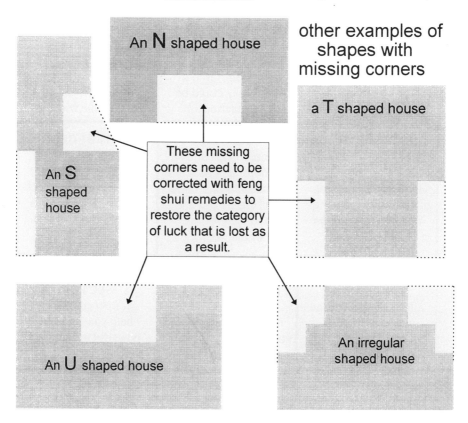

An N shaped house

other examples of shapes with missing corners

a T shaped house

An S shaped house

These missing corners need to be corrected with feng shui remedies to restore the category of luck that is lost as a result.

An U shaped house

An irregular shaped house

The effect of missing corners depends on which corner is missing

There are two excellent methods of diagnosing the effect on the family luck when there are missing corners. The first method relates to the kind of luck affected while the second method describes which member of the family's luck gets affected.

<u>The Pa Kua method</u>
assigns one type of luck to each of the eight corners of any home. To determine the kind of luck affected, it is first necessary to determine which compass direction is represented by the missing sector. Use a good compass to first determine the orientations of your home, then superimpose a nine sector grid onto your house plan. You will see immediately which sector is missing. Then check against the meanings shown in the nine sector grid illustrated below.

SOUTHEAST SECTOR affects wealth luck. if this corner is missing, the income of the family is severely affected in a negative way.	SOUTH SECTOR affects the luck of respect, recognition, and fame. If this corner is missing, the good name of the family could be tarnished.	SOUTHWEST SECTOR affects luck associated with love, romance and marriage. If this corner is missing, love flies out the window.
EAST SECTOR A missing corner in the East affects family relationships and health, causing misunderstandings and sickness.	CENTER If there is an empty atrium, unless it is decorated and used will create severe bad luck for the whole family.	WEST SECTOR A missing corner in the West reduces the luck of the next generation. Children luck will be badly affected .
NORTHEAST SECTOR affects the knowledge luck of the family. Students taking exams or applying for jobs will have no luck.	NORTH SECTOR affects your career prospects. A missing corner here blocks your chances of upward advancement.	NORTHWEST SECTOR severely curtails the help you get from powerful mentors. A missing corner here is very bad luck !

A missing northwest corner severely affects the fortunes of the family patriarch or breadwinner

Perhaps more important than the type of luck affected is the effect which missing corners have on the luck of each individual member of the family, based on the Trigram method

The most dangerous missing corner is the corner represented by the direction **Northwest** which is the house of the trigram *chien* which represents the most senior male member of the family - usually the father or patriarch. If the northwest corner is missing (or if it houses a frequently used toilet, a store room filled with junk, or a cluttered garage) the luck of the father could be seriously affected. If he is also the sole breadwinner, then such a situation affects the whole family since his career and his business ventures will suffer from a lack of energy and motivation on his part. Here is the full table of meanings.

SUN in the SOUTHEAST affects the eldest daughter	**LI in the SOUTH** affects the middle daughter	**KUN in the SOUTHWEST** affects the matriarch or mother
CHEN in the EAST affects the eldest son	The center affects the whole family	**TUI in the WEST** affects the youngest daughter
KEN in the NORTHEAST affects the youngest son	**KAN in the NORTH** affects the middle son	CHIEN in the NORTHWEST affects the father

There are easy feng shui cures for missing corners

There several solutions which can be used to correct the effects of missing corners, and which method you use depends on your budget as well as your space constraints.

For homes with gardens and where there is no space constraint, the best way is to literally build an extension which regularizes the overall shape, transforming an **L** shape home for instance into a rectangular shaped home. The same can be done for **U** shaped and **N** shaped homes. You can add a room, or if this is too expensive you can simply landscape the corner with plants and stepping stones, capped by a tall light in the corner thereby visually *stretching* the corner out. This is shown below.

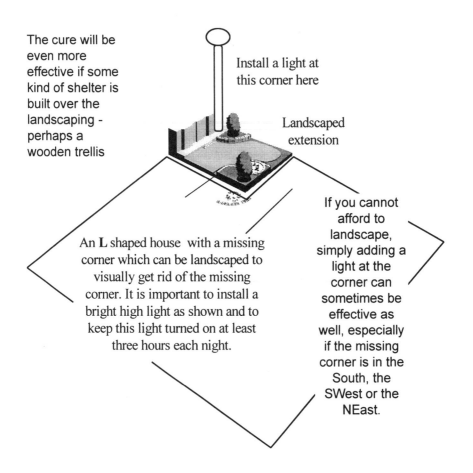

The cure will be even more effective if some kind of shelter is built over the landscaping - perhaps a wooden trellis

Install a light at this corner here

Landscaped extension

An **L** shaped house with a missing corner which can be landscaped to visually get rid of the missing corner. It is important to install a bright high light as shown and to keep this light turned on at least three hours each night.

If you cannot afford to landscape, simply adding a light at the corner can sometimes be effective as well, especially if the missing corner is in the South, the SWest or the NEast.

If your missing corner is inside an apartment the best cure is to use a full wall mirror

If you do not have a garden because you live in an apartment, the only way to extend a missing corner is to use a wall mirror.

This solution however should only be used if the mirror does not need to be placed inside a bedroom. It is important to always remember that in solving one feng shui problem, you do not inadvertently create another, bigger problem, and having a mirror wall inside a bedroom creates a great deal of unsettling energy which can be most inauspicious !

Missing corner

In this one bedroom apartment, which is **U** shaped, the missing corner is very small, and can usually be ignored. However if it happens to be located in one of the compass directions that represent a category of luck considered significant to the resident's aspirations, the missing corner should be addressed. The solution then is to install a full length wall mirror on either wall where the dotted line has been drawn in …this will have the effect of visually stretching out the wall …

In using wall mirrors in the home for whatever reason there are several guidelines which should be strictly followed.

1. Full wall mirrors should be high enough so that it does not cut off the full reflection of the tallest member of the household.
2. Mirrors should also not cut off the feet of residents.
3. Never place mirrors that directly reflect a toilet, a staircase, the kitchen stove or oven, or worse of all, the main door.
4. Never install wall or other mirrors in the bedroom directly facing the bed. This will be a serious mistake that could cause severe harm to a marriage if the mirror is in the main bedroom, and generally cause sleepless nights for everyone affected by the mirror.
5. Mirrors are excellent in the dining room as it doubles the food on the table BUT not in the kitchen !

Protruding corners strengthens the luck of the corner and the effect can be auspicious

Sometimes when extensions are added to the home, the luck of the corner and that of the family member represented can be enhanced. However, extensions that stick out must also be analyzed according to the *element* attribute of the shape of the extension, and care must be taken that this element is in a balanced relationship with the *element* of the main shape of the home. To undertake this analysis, it is necessary to study the element relationships explained fully in a later section of this chapter.

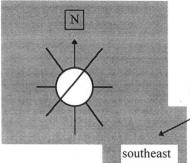

southeast

The extension here strengthens the SE corner of the home. This is excellent for wealth luck and benefits the eldest (or only) daughter of the family. It is also not too large as to overwhelm the main house.

The extension here is in the West corner, and this benefits the children luck of the family. Those having a hard time starting a family could consider this as an excellent feng shui feature which could help. The West also benefits the youngest daughter of the family.

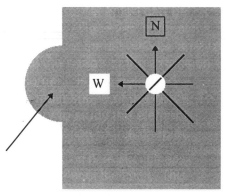

Note also in the examples above,

1) a rectangle added to another rectangle is balanced and there is no problem of the elements clashing since the extension and the main part of the house has the same shape.
2) In the second example a semi circle has been added to a rectangle. The rectangle is of the *earth element*, while the semi circle is of the *metal element*, and since *earth produces metal* in the cycle of *element relationships*, once again the extension is harmonious.

Shapes have *element* attributes which in turn have feng shui implications

There are five basic shapes which have element significance and these offer clues for analyzing the suitability of the shapes to the usage of the buildings.

Square or rectangular shapes represent the EARTH element, and are usually the most suitable for residences. Square or rectangular shapes offer support, security and stability - all of which are attributes associated with the earth element. The square shape also lends itself easily to feng shui enhancements that are based on compass school formulas, and are thus highly recommended as the best shape to use.

squares belong to the earth element

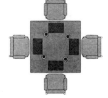

A square shaped dining table reflects the stability of the earth. It is an excellent shape for a small family. Just make sure that the sharp corners of the table do not point directly at any important door.

A square shaped house seen from the ground also suggests stability. The energies associated with such a shape are balanced, and therefore auspicious. Such homes should not however have any of the water associated colours like blue or black as dominant colors.

Round structures such as public water tanks, or planetariums send out strong energies associated with the metal element. It thus represents gold or money which is why the Chinese are so fond of **round dining tables !** The round shape also represents heaven. Semi circle extensions are also regarded as auspicious although it being a half circle, it suggest something incomplete.

circular shapes belong to the metal element

The round shape is not recommended for homes, but they can be auspicious for banks and other financial institutions.

29

A vertical rectangular shape represents the wood element

Shop houses such as these also suggest growth as a result of the **wood** element of their shape.

Buildings which are strongly rectangular are extremely auspicious since **wood** suggests growth, power and healthy continuing success. When the color green dominates the auspicious effect is further magnified.

Such shop houses of the old days are auspicious for another reason - they are usually deep, suggesting prosperity for a very long time.

The wood shape which is an elongated rectangular shape is considered to be very auspicious. This shape is suitable for both domestic residences as well as large corporate buildings and commercial developments like warehouses, factories, cinemas, and shopping complexes.

Two examples of triangular fire shape buildings

Triangular shaped buildings symbolize the rising fire energy. Such buildings are usually too strong for most people since the *yang* energies are too dominant. They are suitable for temples and places of worship

The Sydney Opera House has a fire element roof line that is excellent for the building's usage.

Other common shapes may be lucky or unlucky based on symbolic associations

According to certain feng shui masters, shapes can also be considered auspicious if they resemble Chinese characters which have good meanings. At the same time, the way shapes are combined also have lucky or unlucky meanings.

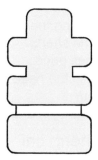

This shape on the left resembles the Chinese character *Ji* which means luck, so it is considered as auspicious

This shape on the left looks like the Chinese word *Wang* which means king so it too is auspicious !

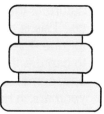

These two shapes on the left on the other hand are considered to be inauspicious since they resemble the Chinese words *Xia*, which means down, and *Xiong* which means bad luck !

Xia

Xiong

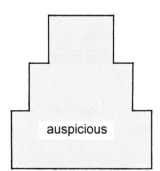

auspicious

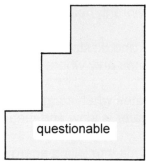

questionable

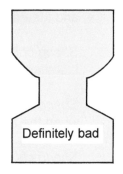

Definitely bad

A building that gets smaller as it gets higher is said to resemble an upward pointing arrow. It is therefore auspicious

A building that looks like steps can be interpreted as good because energy movement seems to be upwards. But something seems to be missing.

A building which has its belly cut up like this cannot possibly be auspicious !

Homes benefit from the dragon's cosmic breath

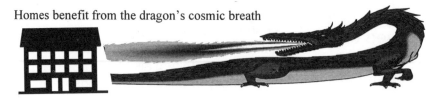

The third important concept of feng shui is in understanding the nature of the dragon's cosmic breath, what is termed the *sheng chi.* This is described as the <u>intrinsic energy</u> which brings good fortune. Every feng shui recommendation has its roots in the need to capture this auspicious energy which is present in our environments when the *elements* are in balance and when *yin* and *yang* are in harmony.

Sheng chi is also present in abundance wherever the *green dragon* resides. This, as we have seen is colorfully described as environments where the natural landscape is conducive to good feng shui. Dragons cannot live where the *chi* scatters or dissipates; or where it stagnates and gets stale.

Sheng chi is created and can accumulate in abundance in places where breezes blow and the energy is vibrant, healthy and alive.

Sheng chi scatters where winds blow too fast but halts and accumulates when it meets slow moving water

Sheng chi scatters and dissipates when the wind blows too fast. It settles and expands only where winds are gentle.

Sheng chi evaporates when caught in a raging river, but halts when the flow of water is slow and meandering.

Sheng chi transforms into killing energy when forced to move too fast, or in a straight line. But it stays benevolent when allowed to meander. The correct flow of *sheng chi* brings immense good fortune, and where ever it has a chance to amass and collect, the abundance is greatly magnified.

To create good feng shui therefore, it is vital to understand the nature and flow of *sheng chi.*

The flow of *chi* in the natural landscape is affected by the shape and orientation of mountains, hills and rivers

When you understand the way the invisible energy in the atmosphere moves and flows, you will begin to understand how these energies can be beneficial or harmful. When we speak of *sheng chi* we are referring to the good energy, and the way this energy drifts and ebbs within the environment is influenced by the shape, contour and elevation of the land ... hill and mountain ranges as well as rivers, lakes and vegetation all affect the quality and currents of *chi* in the atmosphere. At the same time man made structures introduced into the environment also affect the flow of *chi.*

Man made structures also affect the flow of chi

When the structure that is built blends in with the natural surroundings, the flow of good *sheng chi* can even get enhanced, but when discordant notes are created, the *sheng chi* becomes killing or *shar chi*. As a result, the feng shui surrounding new buildings can be negatively affected, and worse, the feng shui of the entire area gets spoilt thereby affecting other houses in the area.

The cardinal rule is never to introduce sharp, angular or gigantic structures that cut into dragon hills, or create massive soil erosions that affect drainage and water flows.

Leveling the range of hills here is like injuring the dragon ... and worse, ti takes away the back support for the building, thereby transforming good *sheng chi* into harmful *shar chi*

Orientating the massive buildings to have their backs supported by the mountain range would have been a better idea than leveling off the mountain behind. By exposing the building to the elements in this way, occupants of the buildings cannot benefit from the flow of *chi.*

In cities, and other urban areas, buildings become *mountains,* and roads take on the energy flow of rivers

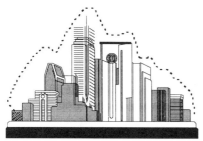

In cities and urban environments, buildings can be substituted for elevated land forms while roads and highways are the modern equivalents of rivers.

The same rules apply equally in cities as in country environments. *Chi* must be allowed to slow down, meander, revolve and accumulate. It should not become stale by stagnating; nor should it move too fast so that it is forced to scatter and disperse.
How are these theoretical guidelines to be applied to our homes and our living space ?
By understanding the way *chi* moves and circulates.

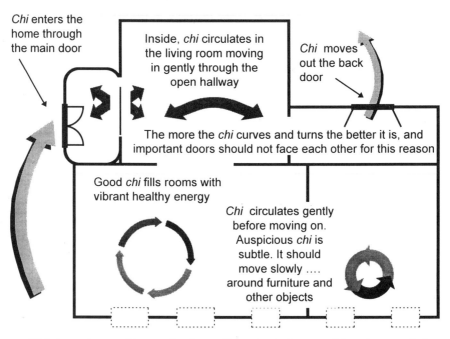

Chi enters the home through the main door

Inside, *chi* circulates in the living room moving in gently through the open hallway

Chi moves out the back door

The more the *chi* curves and turns the better it is, and important doors should not face each other for this reason

Good *chi* fills rooms with vibrant healthy energy

Chi circulates gently before moving on. Auspicious *chi* is subtle. It should move slowly …. around furniture and other objects

Chi also enters and leaves the home through windows, and the placement of windows relative to doors become significant since it affects the flow of *chi.*

The principles of *chi* flow can be applied to the roads round you, and to the way you orientate your home

The road facing this house appears to **cut** the house. *Chi* is moving too fast. It is hostile and most inauspicious.

By the time the *chi* flows down to the front of this house it has turned benign; Having slowed down, it gently **embraces** the house. This type of road is thus auspicious.

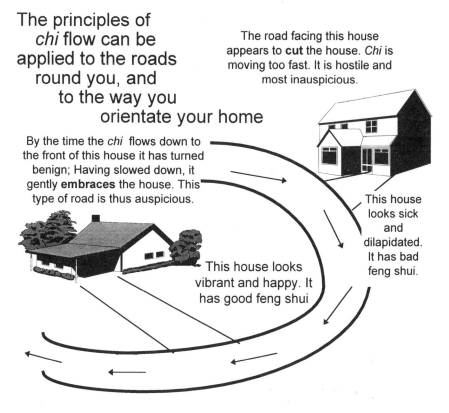

This house looks sick and dilapidated. It has bad feng shui.

This house looks vibrant and happy. It has good feng shui

Here is a short summary of ground rules to assist you develop feng shui *eyes*. They should help you develop an awareness of your surroundings. It is necessary to practice this awareness before moving on to other feng shui concepts, and before starting to practice compass formula feng shui.

- Do not live in a dead end. Here *chi* stagnates, and when you have problems, there will be no way out …
- Do not live sandwiched between two buildings which dwarf your home. The buildings block any benevolent chi from flowing into your home.
- Do not live with your main door directly facing a straight road. The chi flowing towards you will be too powerful.

- Do not have your main door , or the front of your home, face higher ground, a large building or a wall. This blocks off the *chi*.
- Do not live in a home that has a fast moving highway, or a river at the back. The *chi* is too powerful and there will be nothing guarding your back.
- Do not live too near to road flyovers which seem to cut into your home or the building that houses your apartment. The *chi* turns lethal.

Just as there is benign breath surrounding us, there is also the hostile breath - what in feng shui is termed *shar chi*, which is translated as killing breath. Much of feng shui practice has to do with deflecting, dissolving and dispersing this *shar chi*. This fourth conceptual principle is a most vital dimension in the practice of feng shui. It is more important to guard against *shar chi* than to focus only on enhancing feng shui. This is because all the most excellent feng shui features introduced into the home will be powerless against the killing force of severe *shar chi* . **It is vital to guard against shar chi** This is why I always start my feng shui analysis by looking at the overall surroundings. I know how important it is to determine that the big thing must first be made right before going on to the other aspects of feng shui practice.

Shar chi caused by landscape orientations are very lethal, and difficult to cope with; more so than the *shar chi* caused by incorrect arrangements of furniture inside a home. This is why, when you select your permanent home, you should be so careful.

Choose your neighborhood carefully

Look out for the tell tale signs of prosperity. Investigate the history and background of people already living there. Usually, when an area, or a building has good feng shui, the place will actually look prosperous. The gardens will be thriving, the houses will be well maintained, the streets will be relatively clean, and there will be an air of prosperity which you will be able to feel if you tune yourself to the energies of the area.

Look at this threatening arrow. This is what *shar chi* feels like, something threatening and aimed directly at your home.

When an area is suffering from massive doses of *shar chi* you will see it manifested in the dilapidated condition of the homes and buildings in the area. This is how the slums of cities get created. Corrupt energy makes an area get poorer and poorer, and less and less healthy. Sometimes the cause of the *shar chi* is not immediately obvious. When you look hard enough however, the cause will usually be a massive threatening feature poised like a secret arrow emanating lethal energies outwards.

Looking out for poison arrows that shoot out massive doses of *shar chi*

Looking out for *shar chi* is a big part of feng shui. There are many things in the environment that can cause *shar chi*, and take on the guise of poison arrows BUT one should not become paranoid.

Even as you keep an eye out for potentially harmful structures around your home, remember that nothing that is not directly hitting your front, and especially your main door, can harm you. Plus, there is always a solution to any feng shui problem. But first here are the some very basic things to commit to memory.

One **Never ever let your front door directly face a structure that is larger than your house. And never live in a building that is similarly afflicted. Here are some examples illustrated.**

edge

An imposing building, particularly the edge of the building. The nearer the building is to you, the more harmful it is. If it is half a mile away, it does not harm you. If your home faces such a building, try to change its orientation such that the building is behind you. This implies changing your door, but drastic problems call for drastic solutions. Turn this evil monster in front of you into a benign protector behind you !

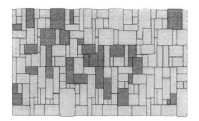

A neighbor's massive wall, if it is higher than the ground level of your home (and worse if it is higher than that), you have a problem. Try using another door as your main door. Or use plants with plenty of foliage to block off at least part of the wall.

A clock tower   a cross

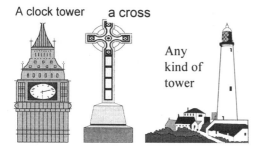

Any kind of tower

Anything tall, straight and huge in front of you is bad news. This sort of structure causes massive amounts of *shar chi.* You need a powerful Pa Kua mirror, which may not even be strong enough. So how about a cannon ?

Two **Watch the roads around you. Strenuously avoid living:**
- **at the end of a straight road - the notorious T junction**
- **next to a road flyover**
- **on the cutting edge side of a curved road**
- **below the road level**
- **facing a Y**

A Y junction, pointed at the main door is a problem which can be corrected by planting a hedge. This visually blocks off the offending junction.

The T junction is deadly. Block it off with a wall, a hedge or a clump of trees.

Three Look out for the neighbor's triangular roof line, the garbage across the road, single trees, lamp posts, telephone poles, street signs pointed at your door. These poison arrows are less severe than the first two categories and are also easier to deal with. Block them off from view, or divert the *shar chi* elsewhere with a wall or hedge.

Be careful about the angular roof line of your neighbor's house. This is a serious poison arrow. If it directly hits at your front door use a Pa Kua mirror to counter. Make sure you do not build a house that has a roof line pointed at someone else's home. Remember that when they retaliate with a Pa Kua, the poison arrow rebounds back at you !

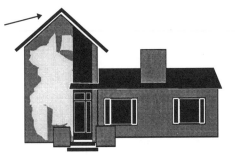

Central to the understanding of many feng shui rules and recommendations is the concept that all physical things, all intangible energy, all directions and all seasons possess *element* attributes that relate mutually to each other. The nature of this interaction is what creates

The five elements are fire, water, metal, earth, and wood

harmony or disharmony in any area. This is the fifth basic concept which should be committed to memory as it provides you with the explanation that lie behind so many feng shui correcting and enhancing techniques. The reference grid below summarizes the direction and other associations of the five elements.

SOUTHEAST	SOUTH	SOUTHWEST
the element of **small** WOOD associated with the color light GREEN young growing plants anything rectangular the season of spring expanding energy	the element of **FIRE** associated with the color RED the bright sunlight the glow of lamps anything sharp or pointed the season of summer upward rising energy	the element of **big** EARTH associated with the color OCHRE stones and pebbles boulders and crystals in between seasons sideways moving energy
EAST the element of **big** WOOD associated with the color dark green full grown plants flowers and seeds the season of spring outward flowing energy	The center is of the **EARTH** element	**WEST** the element of **small** METAL associated with the color white with gold and silver the season of autumn inward flowing energy
NORTHEAST the element of **small** EARTH associated with the color beige the soil, the earth anything square in between seasons horizontal moving energy	**NORTH** the element of WATER associated with the colors BLACK/BLUE the season of winter anything wavy in shape the season of winter meandering energy	**NORTHWEST** the element of **big** METAL associated with all metallic colors gold and silver the season of autumn inward flowing energy

The **FIRE**
element

Elements attributed to
each of the
compass directions
tells you how to energize
all the corners of
your home and office

Fire is associated with the
South, so when placed in
the South corners of
rooms and homes, it brings
soaring energy. Lights in
the South part of the
garden and in a foyer of
the home that is placed
South attract upward rising
chi flow that bring success,
fame and recognition to the
residents.

Fire energy
always
indicate
success
associated
with public
recognition

When the fireplace is located along the
South wall of your living room, the fire
energy creates perfect *yang* energies that
counter the excessive *yin* energies of the
winter months. A fire place in the South
also activates success luck for the family.
During summer months when the fire
place is not in use, place a lamp on the
mantelpiece above the fireplace.

The nature of the FIRE element can be extremely powerful so
treat it with respect. Those born in the years of this element (see
tables at the back of this book) have a particular affinity with fire
because this is their natural element. Snake or Horse year people
also have an affinity to the fire element. Do not forget the
importance of balance. There should never be too much of any
single element, so do keep the fire under control. When the moon
is full, the fire element becomes extremely strong. The same
happens during the summer months. Once fire reaches its
maximum potential, as in the cold months) it will start to diminish,
and when it does, artificially created fire element like bright lights
and burning candles compensate for the waning fire energy.

When *playing with fire* also remember the cycles of the elements
dealt with a little later. Always take note that the element of wood
fans the fire, while the element of water extinguishes it .

The **WATER** element is associated with the <u>North</u>. So anything that suggests it, placed in the North activates the energy of water. Water energy moves downwards; it represents the new moon, the beginning of a cycle. Dark colors - black or blue - represent this element. To activate water use dark blue carpets and curtains, as well as upholstery, duvet covers and scatter cushions which have dominant blue colors.

Use blues and blacks to represent water in the North

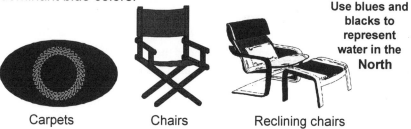

| Carpets | Chairs | Reclining chairs |

Household furnishings provide excellent mediums for activating the elements. Play with colors, and benefit from feng shui inspired creation of harmony by matching the colors with the correct corners of any room.

Those born in water element years feel comfortable with the water element, as do those born in Rat or Boar years. But as always, never go overboard with water, or it could drown you. Do not have too much. Remember that in feng shui, the practice of manipulating the energies in the surroundings should be very subtle, and less is always better than more.

The best method of energizing the wonderful essence of the water element is to install an aquarium with bubbling oxygenated water. Keep good luck fish like carp, goldfish and guppies ...

Introducing a water feature in the North brings wonderful CAREER luck !

It is an excellent idea to activate the water element in the garden, if you are lucky enough to have one. Introduce a small fountain; or if you have a big mansion and a big budget, create an artificial waterfall. Place it in the **North** part of your garden, OR place it somewhere in full view of your main door. But make sure it is on the left hand side of the garden !

The **WOOD** element

Wood symbolizes expansion, epitomized by the happiness of springtime, when plants germinate and start to grow. Of the five elements, wood is the only one with a life of its own. Wood represents the waxing moon, gathering strength and radiance with each passing day. Its energies radiate outwards in all and every direction, like the branches of a tree. Wood is the direction of the East, the abode of the green dragon where the element of wood takes on the form of a tall and imposing tree. It is also the element of the Southeast, the place of small wood - the place also that represents material wealth. Activating the wood corners of the home brings great benefits, and especially for those born in wood years or in the years of the Tiger or the Rabbit - both of which astrological signs also belong to the wood element. Use every kind of plant (even artificial ones work, but not dried plants or flowers) except those with pointed leaves or sharp thorns. All forms of cactus should never be placed inside the home. And bonsai plants - which are artificially stunted are not very suitable either.

Place medium sized plants along the East walls of your home to simulate the element of big wood. In the garden, a large tree with spreading branches and good foliage is also effective. The pine tree and the bamboo also represents longevity so you can take your pick !

Creepers and vines are excellent to camouflage any ugly sights and structures which you may have in the East or Southeast part of your home or garden. Creepers are also great for softening the hostile energies of sharp edges and protruding corners. If the vines produce beans, place them in the SEast to symbolize a good harvest !

Flowering plants are excellent in the Southeast. When plants bloom, they bring wonderful vibrant energy associated with success. The Chinese always describe a successful life as one that has started to blossom. Since the SEast represents wealth, flowers here are most suitable.

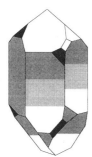

The **EARTH** element

The earth element epitomizes the core of feng shui. Powerful earth energy moves sideways and horizontally, spreading its essence each time the seasons start to change - aiding the transition from summer to autumn to winter to spring and back to summer once again. The EARTH element is associated with the <u>Southwest</u> which represents big earth , and also the <u>Northeast</u> where the element is small earth. The center of a home is also considered to belong to the earth element. In all these sectors of the home, or in the SW and NE of the garden, strengthening the earth element brings great harmony of energies.

Be especially focused on the center because creating harmonious energy in the center brings good fortune to the whole family. It also helps in fostering good relationships between siblings.

Crystals are splendid symbols of the earth element. Both natural crystals and man made crystals are equally effective. Place them in the **Southwest** corner of your living room to energize romance luck, and in the **Northeast** to help in the attainment of educational success.

other symbols of the earth element include things made of clay or ceramics & pottery

Ceramic tea pots and vases also make great earth element energizers.

Large decorative urns and water vessels make excellent energizers for the earth corners of a home

Choose those which also have good fortune symbols painted on them - these can depict the mou tan flower or peony which is excellent for the SW; or any of the longevity symbols like the crane, pine trees or bamboo to enhance the energies that bring good health luck into the home. In recent years the ceramic industry of China has expanded greatly, and it is not difficult to find some excellent specimens.

A pot of *gold*
is the best
representation
of the **METAL** element

The two
directions that
belong to the
metal element
are **Northwest**
and **West**

In feng shui of course all things are symbolic.
But placing left over change - coins - in a metal container and
placing it in the metal directions, the Northwest or the West
magnifies the energies of the these sectors and adds to the
harmony of the flow of energies within the home. Energies of
the metal element are both dense and inward flowing. Metal is
also associated with gold and silver, and these have always
been the symbols of wealth and prosperity.

Anything metallic like coins and gold
bars are always suitable for metal
corners. Those born in metal years
or in Rooster and Monkey years
have a special affinity with metal.

three
old
Chinese
coins
for
wealth

The best object to use for enhancing metal energies are the
old Chinese coins drawn above. The combination of a
square hole on a round coin symbolize heaven and earth.

Tie three coins together with red thread to energize the
coins, and then place them in the metal corner of your living
room. This is a very powerful method of enhancing
incomes, and there are lots of other ways to use these
coins. These other methods are covered in a later section.
Remember that the red thread is vital since is believed to
be what causes the energies of the coins to be released.

The five elements interact in continuos Productive and Destructive cycles

Understanding the way the energies of the five elements affect one another allows the practitioner to understand what feng shui harmony is all about. Study the cycles presented here carefully to enhance your understanding of feng shui.

There are two major cycles of interaction that govern the relationship of the elements - and these cycles of production and destruction give rise to either harmony or disharmony when they come in contact with one another.

In the productive cycle ...

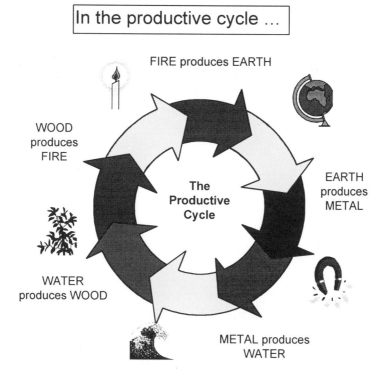

FIRE produces EARTH

WOOD produces FIRE

EARTH produces METAL

The Productive Cycle

WATER produces WOOD

METAL produces WATER

The productive cycles indicate the elements that have a harmonious relationship. Let us use one example. From the cycle above:
WATER is excellent for WOOD because it produces WOOD.
But this means that WOOD exhausts WATER ...
So while Water is good in a Wood sector ,
Wood may not necessarily be good in a Water sector.
Now do your own analysis with the other elements in the Productive cycle, and then apply this principle carefully when you plan the furnishings and placement of objects in the rooms of your home.

The destructive cycle

The destructive cycle shows the elements which are seemingly in direct conflict with each other. The nuances of this discordant relationship however, are subtle, and requires more than superficial consideration. It is necessary to also consider the *size* of the elements.... Thus while METAL is said to destroy WOOD, it depends on whether it is big or small metal, and whether it is big or small wood whose contact we are investigating. This rationalization exercise applies to all elements.

So consider :
Small metal transforms big wood into something of greater value ... as when metal tools and implements turns a piece of log into furniture and works of art !

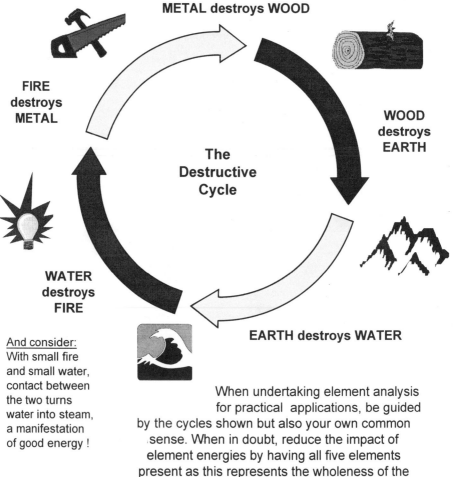

METAL destroys WOOD

FIRE destroys METAL

WOOD destroys EARTH

The Destructive Cycle

WATER destroys FIRE

EARTH destroys WATER

And consider:
With small fire and small water, contact between the two turns water into steam, a manifestation of good energy !

When undertaking element analysis for practical applications, be guided by the cycles shown but also your own common sense. When in doubt, reduce the impact of element energies by having all five elements present as this represents the wholeness of the Universe and is considered auspicious !

Applying element cycles in feng shui practice

The significance of the five elements and their cycles of production and destruction in feng shui cannot be over stressed. The elements are regarded as an intrinsic part of the energies of the earth. The cycles manifest their roles as agents of the earth's dynamic - the continuos process of change caused by, and resulting in, creation and destruction. When you understand the elements, you will appreciate the effect they have on the harmony of the environment. The concept thus becomes an important analytical tool of feng shui practice.

To apply element analysis to your feng shui knowledge, first study the relationships of the elements, noting the nuances that are related to other considerations. Next, commit to memory the element categorization of shapes, seasons, numbers, directions, objects and so forth.
Then systematically identify the elements in each corner of your home, and move them around to achieve harmony by making sure no conflict of elements occur in any corner of your home.
<u>Two examples :</u>
Do not place water in the SOUTH because water destroys the fire element of the South !

And do not put a round extension in the EAST because round is metal and metal destroys the wood element of the East.

	WOOD	WATER	FIRE	METAL	EARTH
season	spring	winter	summer	autumn	between
direction	east/SE	north	south	west/NW	SW/NE
color	green	black	red	white	ochre
shape	rectangle	wavy	triangular	round	square
energy	outwards	descending	upwards	inwards	sideways
numbers	3, 4	1	9	6, 7	2, 5, 8

Do remember however, that what is given here is a simplistic approach. There may be instances when the rules of element cycles may have to be overridden by other considerations.
When in doubt just remember that in feng shui you cannot get everything right. Sometimes you may have to compromise, but in so doing, make sure that the larger landscape considerations always take precedence when you make your judgments.

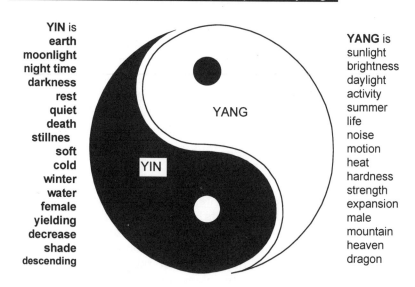

YIN is
earth
moonlight
night time
darkness
rest
quiet
death
stillnes
soft
cold
winter
water
female
yielding
decrease
shade
descending

YANG is
sunlight
brightness
daylight
activity
summer
life
noise
motion
heat
hardness
strength
expansion
male
mountain
heaven
dragon

All the energies of the earth - which can be regarded as synonymous to the breath of the dragon, the *sheng chi* - are said to be either *yin* or *yang*. The cosmology of these two opposing yet complementary forces is the conceptual way the Chinese view the Universe. *Yin* and *yang* have their own attributes and their own magnetic fields of energy. They are different, but are nevertheless dependent on each other. One gives existence to the other. One cannot exist without the other !

The energies around us are deemed to be in a beneficial state of balance when both yin and yang are present. The relative strength of each in any given situation has to be finely tuned according to circumstances, but there should never be so much yin as to completely obliterate yang and vice versa. For <u>yang feng shui</u>, yang energies of course vital, but never to an extent that yin is totally diminished although an excess of yin energies can cause havoc and sometimes bring illness and death. Similarly there will be situations when the balance has to be reversed.

The symbol of yin and yang, shown above, is an eloquent expression of its constantly changing state. Study the attributes associated with YIN and YANG, and much of feng shui begin to make perfect sense.

Feng shui is often deemed good or bad depending on the yin and yang balance of the space and its surroundings ...

Exposure to the glare of the western sun cause an excess of yang energy. Too much noise, too much activity, too much brightness are all symptoms of excessive yang energy.

When there is too much shade, and too much stillness. When the nights and the daytimes are cold and lifeless, then the energy is deemed to be excessively yin. Such areas lack life, growth and expansion. Yin places are suitable for the dwellings of the dead, not of the living.

Yin and yang interact continuously, and in the process creates change. Thus, summer (*yang*) reaches its zenith and then starts to fade into Winter *(yin)* before becoming summer once more. Day follows night. The moon gives way to the sun, and darkness becomes light. Everything in the Universe contains varying quantities of *yin* and *yang* energies. In the natural landscape, *yin* and *yang* is expressed by the shape and contours of the terrain, the ground temperatures and the amounts of sunlight and shade.

Look out for yin yang imbalance in your surroundings and correct them

Landscapes that are completely flat are too yin, and require the balance of boulders and plants. Perspectives that have too much exposure to sunlight could be too *yang,* plants here will create shade. A water feature also introduces *yin* energies to create good balance. Look at Japanese and Chinese gardens which are always balanced with *yin* and *yang* lines. Now think of the snowcapped regions of the Poles - altogether too *yin*, think also of hot deserts, altogether too *yang* - such places cannot even attract people to live there, let alone have good feng shui.

Inside the home, *yin yang*
influences the flow of energy
When there is severe imbalance,
especially with too much *yin*
the feng shui of the home suffers

Pets bring precious yang energy

If your home is too quiet, and
the rooms are dark and cold, let
your walls have a new coat of
paint. Make it bright and light.
Keep the radio turned on even
when you are at work,
and keep a pet !

Dogs and cats and even an
aquarium of fish in bubbling water
attracts precious yang energy.

Counter an excess of yin
with bright lights
music and noise …
and keep a pet !!

Counter excess yang
by adding dark colors
dimming the lights
and keeping the curtains
permanently closed

A house which is too yin is not
suitable for most people because
we need lively *yang* energy to
stay fit and healthy. A house
which is too *yang* however,
dissipates our energy

Changes in the seasons affect yin yang balance in the home, so
be alert. When it is cold, foggy and rainy, the skies are dominated
by *yin* energies. Keep your lights and your music turned on.
When the sun shines brightly, and it is a hot sunny day, turn on
the fan and the airconditioners. Of course this is common sense,
but not many people live in such a state of awareness as to
always be conscious of the nuances of the surrounding energy.
If you live in the temperate countries be alert to temperature
changes of the seasons. If you live in the tropics, counter periods
of hot, dry tropical sunshine with *yin,* and rainy spells with *yang.*
The changes may be subtle but feng shui is a very subtle
science. Develop your senses till it becomes second nature !

It is not only on feng shui that the Chinese speak in the language of symbols. Every old tradition, superstition, medical belief, divinitive science and fortune telling are based on ancient symbols, the most important of which are closely associated with the Chinese view of the constantly changing Universe and its philosophy of balance and harmony.

The language of feng shui is very symbolic

There are symbols of the yin and yang cosmology, of the trigrams, the series of broken and unbroken lines that make up the insignia of the ancient classic - the I Ching. We also have the eight sided octagonal Pa Kua symbol, and the nine sector Lo Shu magic square of numbers, and most of all we have the symbolism of the four celestial animals - the dragon, the turtle, the tiger and the phoenix. These have become the interpretative tools of this ancient practice, and each are dealt with separately because understanding them is so important.

There are other symbols which offer further nuances to the practice of feng shui. Some of these are related to the physical manifestations of the five elements, while others signify the whole gamut of life aspirations - longevity, conjugal happiness, fruitful marriages, achieving recognition and authority, and achieving wealth and prosperity and so forth amongst a very long list.

The crane symbolizes longevity

Indeed, the Chinese ascribe so much power to symbols that we have an whole pantheon of Deities which we place in our homes, not for worship, but because they signify wealth, health or happiness. Thus we have the Gods of Longevity, of Wealth, of Happiness, and we have the three star Gods, not to mention classical heroes who have been deified because of the virtues they represent.

We place these deities in our homes in the belief that their presence creates the energies necessary to attract the luck they represent into our homes ! If you are a Chinese and wish to invite say, the God of Wealth into your home, make sure you tie a red string at the base of the statue since this supposedly activates the energies of prosperity !

51

Chinese homes
are filled with paintings
and ceramics that
symbolize all sorts of
good fortune

A pair of mandarin ducks
symbolize happiness in love

Mandarin ducks (they can be made of wood) should be kept in a
pair in the romance corner of the occupants of a home, or in the
universal love corner - the South West.

Paintings that show ideal landscapes, waterfalls, good fortune
fruits and flowers, longevity symbols as well as the Chinese
characters for the words **Luck** or **Growth** or **Prosperity** are all
popular. These symbols of good fortune should be placed in the
corners of rooms according to feng shui guidelines in order to
maximize their promise.

Thus *cranes* and other symbols of longevity can be placed in the
west, which is the corner of the home most suited for the elderly
members of the family. Young growing children can be placed in
the east where the element is wood which signifies growth. Here
the symbol to assist them will be those that signify educational
honors - like a symbolic *jade belt* or simply a healthy growing plant
with branches sent out in all directions.

The color red is
always symbolic
of happiness

It has become a cultural tradition for us to
dress in red, and to offer oranges and red
packets during the lunar new year
because oranges symbolize gold, and the
color red is believed to be an auspicious
color to greet in the new year.

Oranges symbolize gold because the
Chinese word *kum* also means gold.
Peaches signify long life. **Pomegranates**
signify plenty of children and **Lai Chees** and
Longans signify a sweet life.

Good luck flowers are the **plum blossom**, the
chrysanthemum, the **orchid**, and the king of all flowers - the
peony. Good luck trees are the **pine** and the **bamboo** and all
kinds of **blossoms.** These usually signify longevity.

Further symbols believed
to attract good luck are
the eight treasures
shown on this page

The eight treasures are believed to exude excellent good energies for homes. Place them in any corner of your room according to the element of what they are made of.

The **double fish** symbol wards off evil intentions and is sometimes even worn as an amulet. Place it near the entrance of the home.

The **Lotus** brings every kind of good luck. Grown in the home it turns bad luck to good luck !

The **conch shell** attracts travel luck. Place it in the living room.

Jars placed near the entrance of homes attract chi to settle and accumulate.

The **Wheel of Law** represents the power of heavenly energy. A painting of this symbol affords protection.

The **fan** is again an excellent protective symbol for the home.

The **umbrella** or **canopy** is a wonderful symbol of protection. It is believed to ward of burglars when placed near the front part of the home or lobby.

The **mystic knot** indicates a never ending cycle of good fortune. This is a very popular symbol that is carved onto furniture.

The symbols suggested here are part of the Chinese cultural tradition. For my readers who belong to other cultures, I recommend that you use the good luck symbols of your own tradition. They will work just as well.

The eighth basic fundamental of feng shui practice is the significance of orientations, and these are expressed in terms of compass directions. The direction your house faces, your main door, your back door, and all the doors into important rooms where you spend your time, as well as the direction you face when you sleep, work, and eat - all these have significance on the quality of your feng shui.

IN FENG SHUI WHEN WE REFER TO THE NORTH, WE MEAN THE MAGNETIC NORTH. THIS APPLIES IN THE NORTHERN AND SOUTHERN HEMISPHERES

Although the Luo Pan is the feng shui compass used by Chinese Master practitioners, a standard western compass will do just as well

When deciding on orientations either of two approaches can be applied

The first approach is a generalized one, ostensibly said to be applicable to everyone. This approach is based on the **Canon of Dwellings** - an ancient feng shui classic, parts of which have survived. Under this generalized method, specific directions and locations are recommended for specific doors and specific rooms. According to this manual, the recommended direction for the main door is SOUTH, and the NORTHEAST is said to be inauspicious.

Directions are also dealt with in the **Yang Dwelling Classic** which recommends the following:

- Doors into important rooms should face SOUTH.
- The main door should face SOUTH.
- Kitchen doors should face EAST, not SOUTHWEST.
- Shops and business premises should face SOUTH.
- Shops should not face NORTHEAST/SOUTHWEST.
- Older members should live in WEST rooms
- Children of the family should live in EAST rooms.

The second method
is based on the use of
Compass formulas

The second approach defines auspicious and inauspicious orientations according to either a person, or a building's individual natal charts. This requires the use of different formulas which have to be calculated, and then analyzed before deciding on how a home should be orientated. Not all of feng shui's formulas that deal with compass directions have survived the centuries, but those which have, were passed on to *student disciples*, by old feng shui Masters who fled to Taiwan or Hong Kong from China. Many of these old Masters have passed away, and not many of the present day custodians of these formulas, most of whom make a living out of being feng shui consultants, are prepared to part with what they rightly regard as their trade secrets.

I have been lucky in obtaining several of these formulas from my feng shui teacher or *si fu*, **Mr. Yap Cheng Hai,** who has demonstrated remarkable generosity. Calling upon a nearly thirty year friendship with him, I had successfully persuaded him to allow me to use his formulas in my feng shui books. In agreeing, he is sharing a great deal of his feng shui secrets with the world. Mr. Yap's formulas are very potent and powerful. I have used them throughout my life with great success, as have countless extremely prosperous and influential people here in Malaysia, especially his **birth chart based formula on directions**, which uses the Pa Kua and Lo Shu symbols of feng shui as reference points; as well as his **wealth formula on water feng shui.**

**Feng shui master,
YAP CHENG HAI**

I have written separate detailed books on each of these two formulas. I have also written an explicit text on *flying star* feng shui which is the formula for working out the **natal chart of buildings**. This third formula also addresses the time dimension of feng shui.

The application of *formula feng shui* requires a firm grounding in the basic concepts since there is a certain amount of judgmental interpretation involved. Summarized versions of the formulas are thus given in a later section of this book, and readers may choose from amongst the different methods presented to find procedures most suited to enhancing the feng shui of their homes.

But this should be done only after they have taken defensive measures to protect against the *shar chi* of bad feng shui.

The ninth fundamental of feng shui deals with the influence which **time** exerts on the feng shui of a place. The formula which exclusively addresses the intangible forces of the time dimension is the *flying star* formula - a popular method used extensively in Hong Kong. Flying star feng shui is almost predictive in that it is possible to determine periods of good or bad fortune based on meticulous calculations of the movement of the so called *stars* of the Lo Shu grid. These are the numbers 1 through 9.

Feng shui periods are perceived as cycles of time sequences that recur over different durations. A complete cycle of time is said to last 180 years, and this is divided into three sub periods of sixty years each. Each of these sixty years in turn represents one full cycle of the Chinese calendar. This comprise twelve earthly branches, popularly known as the *animals* of the Chinese astrological sequence, and the heavenly stems, or the more colloquial version, the *five elements*. Thus:

12 animal years X the 5 elements = 60 years.

This system of stems and branches comprehensively signify the interaction of heavenly and earthly forces, and are believed to reflect the destiny of all mankind over time. They have thus been incorporated into feng shui technology. The sixty year cycles are further divided into three 20 year periods, and feng shui analysis based on the flying star method offers a different grid of numbers for each 20 year period.

south

6	2	4
5	7	9
1	3	8

The flying star grid of the present 20 year period, which started in 1984 and will end in the year 2003, is shown in the square on the right. Note that this is the Lo Shu square except that the placement of the numbers around the grid is NOT the same as the *original* Lo Shu. This is because the current grid has the number **7** in the center, instead of the original number **5**.

From the above, we can see that the auspicious locations of any house up to the year 2003 are its NE, SE, and NW sectors - with circled numbers. Sectors South and East are unlucky

As always, **SOUTH** is placed on top as shown. And each of the numbers has a feng shui meaning. Thus the numbers **2** and **5** indicate illness, health problems, loss and accidents. The numbers **2** and **3** together indicate quarrels. The auspicious numbers are **1, 6** and **8**, and also the number **7** because this is the period of **7**.

56

The numbers in the *Lo Shu* grid change in every period, every year, every month, and even every hour !

The theory of *flying star* plots the changing numbers as they *fly* over the different sectors of a room, a house, or a building. Dangerous periods for any sector are when the bad numbers, **2** and **5** or **2** and **3** occur together, caused by the way the numbers *fly* in the period, the year and the month…

The method of calculation, and the theory of how the stars *fly* around one's home each year and each month is difficult to learn, although those of you who wish to make the attempt can get my book CHINESE NUMEROLOGY IN FENG SHUI. My book also teaches you how to calculate the natal chart of your home which involves a deeper analysis, and is hence more accurate.

For the amateur practitioner, it is easier to simply take note of the annual flying stars already calculated out. The table below offers a summary of the auspicious and inauspicious parts of your home for the next ten years. These are expressed as compass direction sectors, and the way to apply this set of information is to check the years when your **main door**, or **master bedroom** are placed in the unlucky sectors to determine your year or years of bad luck. During such times, either move room or use another door during that particular year..

LUNAR YEARS	Illness sectors	Loss sectors	**Quarrel** sectors	**Most Auspicious**	**Good Luck** sectors
1997	West,	Southeast	-	Northeast	SW, South
1998	Northeast	Center	-	Southeast	SW, South
1999	South*	South *, NW	-	**Center**	SE, SW
2000	North	West	-	**Southeast, Northwest**	SW, Center
2001	Southwest	Northeast	**South***	**Center, Southeast**	West Northwest
2002	East *	South*	-	**Center, Southeast, Northeast**	Northwest West
2003	Southeast	North *	**North ***	**Northeast Center**	West
2004	Southwest *	Southwest *	-	Northeast	North, NW
2005	Northwest	Northeast *		**South, West**	North
2006	Southeast *	South, West	-	**East**	North,

* denotes extremely bad luck sector in that year.

Investigate time dimension feng shui by superimposing the Lo Shu grid on your house plan

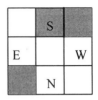

Example: In 1997, the most auspicious sector is **Northeast.** Other good sectors are **Southwest** and **South.** These auspicious sectors are shaded in the grid here. If your master bedroom, main door or other important rooms are in any of these sectors, the time dimension feng shui of your house in 1997 will be good. If your toilet, kitchen or store rooms are located in the lucky sectors, the good luck of these sectors will be wasted. This is determined by <u>superimposing</u> the grid onto your house plans and then taking directions.

Meanwhile, you also know that in 1997, the **West** and the **Southeast** sectors are unlucky sectors. So if your main rooms and main door are located in these sectors, you will suffer some small misfortune or illness. But if your toilets and kitchens are in these sectors, the bad luck get pressed upon !

A wind chime

You can also artificially press down on the bad luck of any sector by <u>hanging a windchime</u> in the area affected. Except that if the bad luck areas are in the East and Southeast, windchimes could clash with the element energy of these two sectors. So in 1997 you can use a windchimes to press the bad luck of the west, but not the bad luck sector of the Southeast.

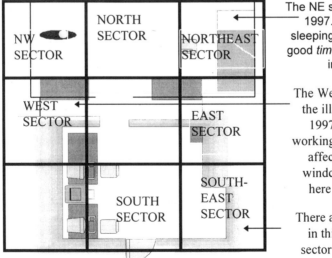

Superimposing the Lo Shu grid on a house plan

The NE sector is lucky in 1997. The person sleeping here will have good *time* feng shui luck in 1997 !

The West sector has the illness star in 1997. Anyone working here will be affected. But a windchime hung here will help.

There are no rooms in this unlucky sector so the time effect is neutral

 **Some basic questions answered**

Question: How do I know if an object is of the wood or fire or water element. And if it is big or small ?
Answer: Basically there are two ways of identifying the element energies of any object. First ask yourself what it is made of, and second ask yourself what it symbolizes. Thus for instance a windchime made of bamboo belongs to *wood*, while one that is made of ceramic is earth and another made of copper or steel is metal. In the same way ask yourself what a globe of the world symbolizes ? Obviously the earth, so it represents the *earth* element. And what does a fish symbolize ? Here the association is water so fish are said to symbolize the *water* element. As to whether it is big or small versions of the element, here, one literally goes by size. A huge oak tree is *big wood*, while a bunch of flowers is *small wood*. A bridge is *big metal*, while a knife is *small metal*.

Question: How do I determine the shape of my house if it is totally irregular, and what if it has combinations of squares, circles and triangles. What perspective do I take - the flat two dimensional layout plan, or the three dimensional elevation.
Answer: You can either artificially separate out the parts and undertake your basic analysis accordingly, or, as recommended by most Master practitioners, take a whole picture view of the entire house shape. Personally, I prefer the whole picture method since this way all I need to do is address any problem of missing corners. The squares, circles and triangles indicate different element energies and you simply check the compass sector to see if the energies are in harmony according to where each of the shapes are located. As to whether you take the two or three dimensional shape, my answer is both.

Both perspectives are important, but if I have to choose which is more important, I would say it is the three dimensional elevation.

Question: How do I know if the yin yang balance of my home is correct ? Do I need to keep rearranging my furniture everytime the season changes ?

Answer: When the energies of yin and yang are well balanced you will feel far more comfortable than if they are not. Some people call this instinctive. That may well be. However, My approach is that all yang dwellings of the living must have more yang than yin energy. The common problem is usually a shortage of yang energy. Or put another way, an excess of yin energy as when your house is badly lit, dirty, cluttered, damp or altogether unhealthy smelling ! Often, in such cases merely opening the windows to let the sunshine in will clear the energies ! Or open all the doors and windows occasionally to bring in fresh energies to replace the stale energies of a place which has been locked up all year. As to whether you need to respond to climatic changes of the season the answer is *yes*, but you do not need to rearrange your furniture. Use lights, fireplaces, and fans to increase or lessen yin and yang energies. As in the practice of anything, there is room for creativity and initiative.

Question: Can I have good feng shui if I only practice the form school basics and ignore the compass school altogether.

Answer: Yes indeed you can. You will also be able to avoid being hit by bad feng shui. But compass school feng shui takes you deeper and allows you to discover powerful methods of seriously enhancing your luck. I always advise my friends to take things one step at a time. Go slowly because it is better to get the basics correct first before trying to apply everything all at once. Besides it is never possible to get feng shui one hundred percent right !

Question: How do I deal with conflicting advice given in different feng shui books ?

Answer: There are many different schools of feng shui. But all authentic feng shui is based on the same concepts. There are some excellent texts out there but there are also some that simply blow my mind ! Perhaps I should add here that so called clearing the energies by clapping your hands and ringing bells is NOT feng shui. The danger in trying to simplify or westernize an ancient Chinese practice is that it can sometimes lead to some hilarious versions of feng shui. I do urge the exercise of good judgment.

3 THE FIVE IMPORTANT TOOLS OF FENG SHUI

The **luo pan** or compass is the basic reference tool used by past feng shui masters. Usually made of wood and painted red, it contains concentric rings of Chinese words that indicate references required for feng shui analysis. Authentic masters had their own luo pans and those purchased off the shops seldom contain the interpretative *secrets* of particular masters' inputs discovered through their years of practice. Such customized luo pans would be unintelligible for those who do not understand the code words used. The standard luo pan contains all the basic concepts related to the practice of feng shui. The circular rows of words refer to trigrams, elements, yin and yang attributes, stems, branches, lo shu numbers and other meanings.

Please remember that although SOUTH is placed at the top, this is only the Chinese convention.

In the center of the *luo pan* is a proper compass which allows the practitioner to get his orientations before proceeding with the feng shui analysis. The needle of the compass is programmed to point SOUTH rather than the conventional NORTH which most of us are familiar with. But this simply follows the Chinese practice of taking their reference point from the South, which is thus always placed at the top.

In practice, the Chinese NORTH is the same magnetic north of Western convention

This DOES not mean that in practice you need to flip the directions. If you have been advised to do this for whatever reason, please note that it is incorrect. I also advise those who live in the Southern hemispheres that there is no need to flip the directions. In feng shui, North is North and South is South wherever in the world you li ʻe.

Today's practitioner of feng shui does not require the *luo pan* compass. Any boy scout or western compass which is accurate and reliable would be more convenient and easier to use. As for the circular rings of meanings which comprise the fundamental concepts for analysis, having a good reference book is sufficient. But it is extremely useful to examine the first few inner circles of the luo pan, and these are far better explained in terms of the eight sided Pa Kua symbol since the meanings are actually derived from the Pa Kua.

For yang feng shui the meanings are derived from the Later Heaven Arrangement of *trigrams* around the Pa Kua.
Shown below however is the Pa Kua of the <u>Early Heaven</u> Arrangement which is used for yin feng shui. This is also the arrangement of trigrams which is used in a
<u>PROTECTIVE PA KUA</u> the Pa Kua which you hang in front of your door OUTSIDE your home to counter shar chi caused by poison arrows which are hitting at your main door.

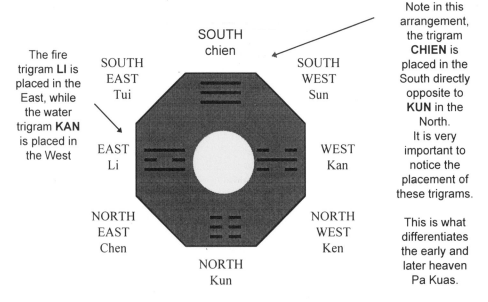

The fire trigram **LI** is placed in the East, while the water trigram **KAN** is placed in the West

SOUTH
chien

SOUTH EAST
Tui

SOUTH WEST
Sun

EAST
Li

WEST
Kan

NORTH EAST
Chen

NORTH WEST
Ken

NORTH
Kun

Note in this arrangement, the trigram **CHIEN** is placed in the South directly opposite to **KUN** in the North.
It is very important to notice the placement of these trigrams.

This is what differentiates the early and later heaven Pa Kuas.

THE PA KUA OF EARLY HEAVEN ARRANGMENT
Used only in yin feng shui analysis

The protective
Pa Kua must be
used very carefully

Never, never
hang it inside
the home

The **Protective Pa Kua** is enlarged on
this page to enable you to trace and make
one of your own in case you need to
counter a poison arrow which may be
sending hostile energies towards you. But
remember that this Pa Kua must never be
hung inside the house.
It must always be HUNG OUTSIDE,
facing away from the house !! Otherwise
the Pa Kua itself becomes a source of
very bad yin death energy.

MAKE YOUR OWN PA KUA
- **Color the background red**
- **Color the trigrams black**
- **Place a mirror in the center**

The Protective Pa Kua
an excellent defensive feng shui tool

The later heaven
   Pa Kua is the one
to use in feng shui analysis

The practice of feng shui requires us to unlock the meanings of the trigrams that are placed around the Pa Kua.

Each of the eight sides represent one of the eight directions. The eight *trigrams* are placed around the Pa Kua, one trigram on each side, according to the later heaven arrangement . This is the arrangement used in yang feng shui analysis. It is these trigrams which assigns the elements and other associations to each of the eight sides, (and therefore the eight directions of the compass). The more important of these associations are shown in the Pa Kua below.

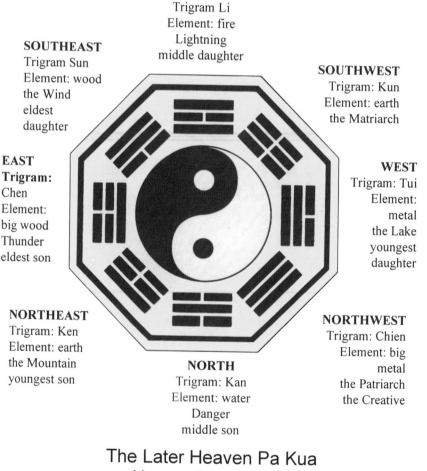

SOUTH
Trigram Li
Element: fire
Lightning
middle daughter

SOUTHEAST
Trigram Sun
Element: wood
the Wind
eldest
daughter

SOUTHWEST
Trigram: Kun
Element: earth
the Matriarch

EAST
Trigram:
Chen
Element:
big wood
Thunder
eldest son

WEST
Trigram: Tui
Element:
metal
the Lake
youngest
daughter

NORTHEAST
Trigram: Ken
Element: earth
the Mountain
youngest son

NORTHWEST
Trigram: Chien
Element: big
metal
the Patriarch
the Creative

NORTH
Trigram: Kan
Element: water
Danger
middle son

The Later Heaven Pa Kua
used in yang feng shui analysis

 **CHIEN** the patriarch also means heaven, the creative, is yang, has metal as the element, and represents the male, the father. The direction is Northwest.

The matriarch **KUN**

Indicates the female maternal, the mother. The element is big earth, the energy is yin. The direction is Southwest .

 CHEN the eldest son

Is in the East, represents wood and the season of Spring. Indicates growth.

TUI youngest daughter

Tui is placed West, and is of the metal element. Tui means joyousness and represents the youngest girl in a home. The season is autumn.

 SUN in the Southeast represents the eldest daughter. The element is wood, the mood is gentle, and the season is Spring. Sun also indicates the wind.

Li stands for fire, with upward moving energy. The season is summer. The trigram symbolizes fame and recognition and intense brightness. **LI** in the South is also the middle daughter

KAN in the North is the middle son

 Kan is the danger trigram. The element is water and the season is deep winter. This trigram also signifies hidden wealth.

KEN the youngest son, placed in the Northeast. Also stands for mountain and belongs to the earth element.

65

The 8 trigrams are the root symbols of the I Ching - and they also reflect the patterns of change over time on the luck of each direction

Those who wish to go deeper into feng shui interpretations can study the I Ching. It is also referred to as the Book of Changes. The I Ching's wisdom is the basis of much Chinese thought and philosophy.

Understanding the meanings of the trigrams leads to many useful applications in feng shui. The placement of the trigrams around the Pa Kua indicates the sectors in a home suitable for each family member. It also tells us which family member is affected when any sector of the home suffers from feng shui afflictions. Examples are missing corners, or a clash of elements to name just two. Similarly, the trigrams also tell us which family member benefits from auspicious energies in the different sectors.

The analysis also goes deeper when we delve into other symbolic representations of the trigrams. Take the example of the trigram KEN which symbolizes *the mountain* in which all sorts of hidden assets (*gold*) may be found. This is confirmed by the element of KEN which is earth, and we know that earth produces metal or gold ! Also, the mountain is big, imposing, silent and still, thus indicating a *period of waiting and preparation*. So if you stay in a room located in the **Northeast,** it might be great while you are a student, but could be frustrating if you are looking for promotion or success luck.

south

The later heaven arrangement of trigrams is shown above with the Pa Kua, the Lo Shu square, and the circular luo pan compass superimposed. This illustrates the layers of meanings that feature in the complete basic practice of feng shui.

Practical applications of trigram therapy in feng shui.
When you understand the attributes of the different corners of any home - its symbolic element, the family member represented, the colours that energize that corner, as well as the luck aspiration symbolized, you can practice trigram therapy in feng shui.

Trigram therapy is a subtle combination of all the nine basic concepts of feng shui and getting it right brings a great deal of harmonious flows of auspicious chi currents that result in good fortune.

In the diagram of the last page, the numbers of the nine sector square - called the lo shu grid - has been superimposed over the pa kua. This represents another layer of associations for the trigrams which can then be incorporated into our basic feng shui practice. Thus every trigram has directions, elements, number and color affiliations. This is summarized below.

The numbers I through 9 shown against the trigrams here are in turn arranged in a certain magic sequence in the Lo Shu. This is shown in the square here. Feng shui texts constantly refer to this arrangement of numbers, and their sequence provides clues to the inner meanings of the trigrams. As such, the numbers of the Lo Shu square have been incorporated into many compass school feng shui formulas.

TRIGRAM	NO	DIRECTION	ELEMENT	COLOR
Chien	6	Northwest	Metal	White
LI	9	South	Fire	Red
Kan	1	North	Water	Black
Chen	3	East	Wood	Green
Sun	4	Southeast	Wood	Green
Kun	2	Southwest	Earth	Ochre
Tui	7	West	Metal	White
Ken	8	Northeast	Earth	Ochre

The numbers of the Lo Shu square are arranged such that any three numbers added up in any direction, always adds up to 15, which is one waxing or waning cycle of the moon. Thus the Lo Shu square features prominently in fortune telling as well as in *flying star*, the time dimension formula of feng shui

The numbers become significant when applying the formulas. But they also indicate the *numerical energy* of sectors eg keep **one** turtle in the North or **4** plants in the Southeast.

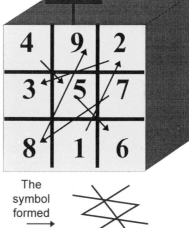

The symbol formed →

Note also the way the numbers move from one to two to three … this movement forms a symbol that closely resembles the *Sigil of Saturn* symbol of the Jewish religion.

There are auspicious and inauspicious dimensions and those who possess what is termed a **feng shui ruler**, can actually measure their tables, cupboards, windows and doors and check if the dimensions are auspicious or inauspicious.

First auspicious segment	First inauspicious sector

The feng shui measuring tape has eight cycles of dimensions, four of which are auspicious and four are inauspicious. Each cycle measures the equivalent of **17 inches or 43 cms**, and each cycle is categorized into eight segments. The cycle of lucky and unlucky dimensions then repeats itself over and over again to infinity. Once you have familiarized yourself with the use of the feng shui ruler you can apply it to almost everything that has a dimension to tap into the auspicious dimensions. In addition to furniture, doors and windows, you can use them also on calling cards, envelopes, notepads, memo paper and so forth. I use them on everything !

The Auspicious
Dimensions

CHAI: which is between 0 and 2 & 1/8 inches or 5.4 cms. This is the first segment of the cycle and it is further subdivided into four categories of good luck. The first approximate half inch brings *money luck;* the second brings a *safe filled with jewels*; the third brings together *six types of good luck*, while the fourth brings *abundance*.

YI: which is between 6 & 3/8 to 8 & 1/2 inches. OR 16.2 cms and 21.5 cms. This is the fourth segment of the cycle. It brings mentor luck ie it attracts helpful people into your life. Again there are four subsections. The first approximate half inch means *excellent children luck*; the second predicts *unexpected added income*; the third predicts a *very successful son* and the fourth offers *excellent good fortune*.

KWAN which is between 8 & /2 to 10 & 5/8 inches OR 21.5 cms to 27 cms. This third set of auspicious dimensions bring power luck and the first sub sector means *easy to pass exams*. The second sub sector predicts *special or speculative luck*, the third offers *improved income* while the fourth attracts *high honors for the family*.

PUN which is between 14 & 6/8 to 17 inches OR 37.5 cms to 43.2 cms. This category of dimensions bring *lots of money flowing in* if it is in the first sub sector. The next sub sector spells *good examinations luck*; the third predicts *plenty of jewelry* and the fourth offers *abundant prosperity*.

The inauspicious dimensions

PI:
which is between 2 &1/8 to 4 &2/8 inches or 5.4 cms to 10.8 cms. This category of bad luck refers to illness. This category also has four sub sectors. The first approximate half inches carries the meaning *money retreats*; the second indicates *legal problems*; the third means *bad luck, even going to jail* !. And the fourth indicates *death of a spouse.*

LI:
which is between 4 & 2/8 to 6 & 3/8 inches or 10.8 cms to 16.2cms. This category means separation and the first half inch means a *store of bad luck* while the second predicts losing money. The third says you *will meet up with unscrupulous people* and the fourth predicts being a *victim of theft or burglary.*

CHIEH:
which is between 10 & 5/8 to 12 & 6/8 inches OR 27 cms to 32.4 cms. This category of bad dimension spells loss. The first approximate half inch spells *death or departure* of some kind; the second that *everything you need will disappear*, and you could lose your livelihood; the third indicates you will be *chased out of your village in disgrace* and the fourth indicates a very *severe loss of money.*

HAI:
which is between 12 & 6/8 to 14 & 6/8 inches OR 32.4 cms to 37.5 cms. These dimensions indicate severe bad luck starting with *disasters arriving* in the first sub sector, *death* in the second, *sicknesses and ill health* in the third and *scandal and quarrels* in the fourth.

The dimensions can be applied to every item in the home although the most important from a feng shui perspective, are doors and windows, beds and tables. I use feng shui dimensions for my calling cards and my books with great success ! Some of the applications are illustrated below.

Office table

DOOR   WINDOW

FLOOR PLANS

<u>Some more basic questions answered</u>

Question: How important is it to fully understand the theory behind feng shui and all the meanings covered in this chapter ?
<u>Answer:</u> It is not easy to understand all the meanings on first reading. You can, if you wish, proceed straight to the later chapters for easy illustrated feng shui tips which you can apply immediately. But when you are unsure, or if the graphic illustrated does not exactly fit your situation, then having the theoretical concepts to refer to become vital. Thus it is not necessary to instantly understand everything. But do try to think things through when you get confused. What I have given in this book is extremely simplified, so you should have no difficulty.

Question: Is the Pa Kua a religious or spiritual symbol ?
<u>Answer:</u> I do not regard it as a religious symbol although I do believe there are spiritual connotations attached to the use of the Pa Kua as a protective symbol. I know that Chinese like to have their Pa Kua blessed at the temple before installing it above their front door. For me personally, I use the Pa Kua only as a last resort. I do not attach any religious or spiritual connotations to it.

Question: What is the significance of the *Sigil of Saturn* symbol formed by the Lo Shu arrangement of numbers ?
<u>Answer:</u> It is a basis for speculating that feng shui as a practice is perhaps related to something similar in the Hebrew & other cultures. I believe that the Chinese do not have exclusive knowledge of this environmental practice which promises so much. Other cultures probably have something similar to feng shui too. Only perhaps not so well documented.

Question: Are there other meanings and associations attached to the trigrams which you have not included in this book ?
<u>Answer:</u> Oh definitely ! If you take the trouble to read the I Ching carefully and study the multiple meanings of the trigrams and hexagrams, you will discover a deluge of information. If you are keen, try to find the Richard Wilhelm translation as it is the most comprehensive. Do not try to study the I Ching from a simplified version. It is much too profound a text for frivolous reading.

4 HARMONIZING
WITH THE OUTSIDE ENVIRONMENT

examining your surroundings

 Your outside feng shui environment is defined as the gardens and roads that surround your home, as well as the full boundary of your vision in all directions. While the limits can sometimes be described as being the space which falls within your visual perimeters, remember that you are also affected by the energy movements in the atmosphere which you may not always see. So when investigating any surroundings with *feng shui eyes* for the first time, the advice is to look up, look down, look in front, look behind, and look sideways.

Be careful of large structures and buildings that cast shadows

> Prevention
> is better than cure
> Look up,
> down, in front
> and look behind

and block off the sun. Look up and see if surrounding hills have threatening shapes or are simply too near. Look skywards to see if you are in the flight path of airplanes. Look sideways to see if electricity substations and transmission lines might perhaps be too near, and try to judge whether future highways, roads and flyovers could well be built nearby. These are all potentially dangerous to your feng shui, and you have to deal with them.

And when you are looking at properties to buy or rent, go even further. Investigate the history of the property. What was the previous land use ? Is it a redevelopment, and if so was there a prison, or a hospital or an execution ground at that site ? If you can, try to avoid living in places which have a bad history.
When looking at land or a new home to buy, do not compromise on the environmental factors. Remember that wrong compass directions are easier to deal with, and correct, than large environmental structures or land forms. It is impossible to move a mountain, and it is hard to combat the *shar chi* caused by gigantic buildings and structures. Or the offensive roofline of a neighbor's house. Or being at the wrong side of a harmful road junction.

When you decide you want to have good feng shui for the place you live, the first thing to do is to look out for structures - buildings, transmission towers, bridges, factory chimneys and so forth - which may be in the vicinity of your home, and to see whether they are hurting your home in anyway. If they are visible but are really very far away, it is not necessary to get unduly worried. The rule of thumb I use is about one li or half a mile distance. But this is only an estimate. The important thing is whether the structure feels threatening to you. Illustrated here and on the next page are some examples of structures that you should be wary of.

Anything tall and straight like a telecommunication Tower can be harmful

Try <u>not</u> to live near a tall structure like the telecommunication tower shown here. You should definitely NOT confront a structure like this; this means you must not directly face it, ie have your main entrance orientated to face it.

CURES
If you are presently facing a tower or a tall building which looks threatening like this, a Pa Kua cannot help much. The best solution is to try and use another door that is<u>not</u> facing the building.

OR if you have a garden, grow a <u>clump of trees</u> with thick foliage and spreading branches to completely block out the view.

From a feng shui perspective, living directly in the shadow of one such tall structure is bad enough but when there are **two such tall buildings in front** of you, they are said to resemble **joss sticks** which send out pernicious yin death energy.

If yours is an apartment that is being hurt, the only way to counter a view of a tower is to use heavy drape curtains that shut out the view completely.

Live away from bridges.
The energy is far too powerful

Traffic patterns around a bridge generates intense movements and concentrations of energy. Houses built at either end of the bridge will suffer from a huge excess of *yang* energy, and residents will be unsettled and unbalanced. There will be so much conflict between themselves. Such a location may be suitable for commerce or entertainment, but domestic residences should not be built near the vicinity of a bridge.

Avoid living near spires and crosses

Don't live near high voltage transmission towers

The energies of high tension wires can play havoc with your feng shui. If you live near these *metallic monsters*, plant strong, high foliage trees between your home and the transmission tower.

Dont face the spires and crosses of a church, these angular features send inauspicious energies your way. Use another door as the main door if you currently have such a problem. The same advice also holds if you live too near a temple. Houses of worship are said to have an excess of yin energy. Living too near them could create imbalance within the surroundings of your home.

Other environmental taboos which you should avoid are:

- living near a dump site. Rubbish heaps are severe bad news !
- living next to an abandoned house. Much too yin !
- living close to graves and hospitals -too near the smell of death
- living next to a police station or a prison. Terribly unbalancing.
- living in the vicinity of polluted drains & canals. Ugh !

Always remember the basic tenets of landscape feng shui

If your home is located in hilly suburbs, then ideally, it should nestle in the bosom of the hills, hugged on the left and right by slightly higher land (with land on the left side being higher), and always supported at the back by higher land. If in the distance behind your home, there is a range of gently rounded hills that are higher, it is excellent feng shui.

If within view of the main door some distance away is a range with three prominent peaks, this means the sons of the family, especially the eldest son will become prominent and successful.

Also take note of landscape taboos

Living directly below an **outcrop of rock** can be dangerous. It is like having something malevolent above you waiting to pounce.

Living at the **edge of a cliff** can be as dangerous. Apart from the obvious dangers, it is also bad feng shui. If the cliff overlooks the sea, the energies are seriously inauspicious. In the illustration here I have also included a lighthouse which is placed on the *tiger* side of House A. The danger for House A is very great. House B has the lighthouse on its dragon side, which affords some kind of protection. But it is still too near the cliff.

Living at the very top of a hill exposes you to fierce wind energies

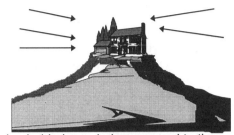

There is little protection when you are at the very top of a mountain ! Planting some trees behind your house may help, but unless there are higher mountains behind you, being exposed to the elements like this will cause your downfall during astrological bad times. It is always better to **live in the belly of the dragon**, ie in the mid levels of hilly ranges. Living at the very bottom is also not advisable since those are areas which could have too much shade. In feng shui it is important to ensure that homes **get enough sunlight.** This brings the auspicious **yang energy** to the houses of the living. But never too much, since this brings an imbalance of the yin and yang requirement. Thus houses on top of hills are never advisable. The problem is made worse of there is also a large body of water built into the compound of the house or condominium.

Remember that water on top of mountain is one of the most dangerous configurations in feng shui.

Water on mountain is most dangerous … Avoid it at all costs

For this reason I always advise friends NOT to have **blue coloured roof tiles.** This imply water on top, which symbolically always means that it overflows.

It is for the same reason that I also strongly advise my rich friends who live in massive penthouses not to build a **swimming pool inside their high rise penthouses.** The effect is like having a home on top of a mountain, with big water there. They could lose their wealth, and their businesses could suffer !

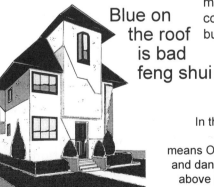

Blue on the roof is bad feng shui

Kan

Ken

CHIEN
**the danger
hexagram**

In the I Ching the hexagram
Chien
means Obstruction. It implies difficulty and danger; water (the trigram KAN) above mountain (the trigram KEN) carries great force and can easily cause damage.

Rivers around you, should **embrace** your home. They should also flow in front of the house, BUT not be flowing directly towards your home, or flowing away from your home. When your house is correctly aligned to tap into the luck of the river, it is extremely good feng shui, but this is not always easy to do. Note some of the taboos illustrated here.

Rivers and views of water should be in front of your house.

Rivers behind create the frustration of missed opportunities

Water is flowing away from the house. How can it bring wealth ?

Water shown below is not merely hitting AT the house; it is also taking wealth **from** the house …

this is because water coming towards the house is narrow, but flowing away it is wide …

All references to rivers apply in the same way to canals, brooks and even roads !

Irrespective of the direction of the water flow, when it passes your front door, the river brings opportunities and wealth. The luck becomes even more auspicious when the water flow direction is harmonious with the direction which your front door faces.

AUSPICIOUS DIRECTIONS OF WATER FLOWS

Remember that directions are always to be taken INSIDE looking out.

Water should flow from left to right when the main door of your house faces North, South, East or West.

Water should flow from right to left when the main door of your house faces Northwest, Northeast, Southwest or Southeast.

Landscape feng shui should be applied wherever you stay

The further away the building is, from your home, the better

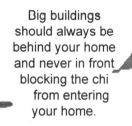

Big buildings should always be behind your home and never in front blocking the chi from entering your home.

1 When there are big buildings around your housing estate, make sure the building is <u>BEHIND</u> your house and NEVER in front !

2 When there is a river or canal near your house, it should flow in front of your house pass your main door, and not behind. If you live in a condominium, the river should flow pass the main entrance of the building. When the water flows at the back of your home, your life will be sorely lacking in success !

3 Land on the left of your house should be higher than land on the right. This conforms to the dragon hills and tiger hills concept of landscape feng shui. And the back of the house must have land higher than in front to provide the vital support.

4 Undulating hilly land is always better than totally flat land. It is only where there are contours and elevations that the symbolic green dragon can have its *lair*. And only such places can be auspicious.

CURES FOR LANDSCAPE FENG SHUI

If you lack a *mountain,* either at the back to represent the support of the turtle hill, or on your left to signify the dragon hill, you can **artificially create a mountain with a mound of earth.**

OR

you can **plant big trees to represent the mountain.** Tall trees with rich foliage are excellent, but remember that they should be at the back of your house or on the *dragon side*. They should <u>never </u>be planted on the *tiger* side as this activates the tiger, and certainly they should not be in front of your house. Trees should support and never block your house !.

Trees make great feng shui cures but they must be used with care

Trees must never be allowed to overgrow or overwhelm the house.

It is just as important to apply classical landscape guidelines to city feng shui as it is to countryside feng shui. The contours of the land around you follow the same rules. Buildings take the place of hills and mountains, while roads are likened to rivers. In addition to the basics which have already been dealt with however, the greater variety of angular shapes, and the elevations of man made structures of the city pose a greater feng shui challenge. Thus we need to look at the buildings around our homes a little more closely.

Building **A** has crosses on its facade, which send out harmful energies.

Buildings in the city come in a variety of shapes and designs and some are more harmful than others

Building **B** has jagged edges pointing outwards. These are most unfriendly.

Building **C** is like a *porcupine* aiming spikes at everyone around it, and its roof catches the sunlight and sends massive **shar chi** outwards.

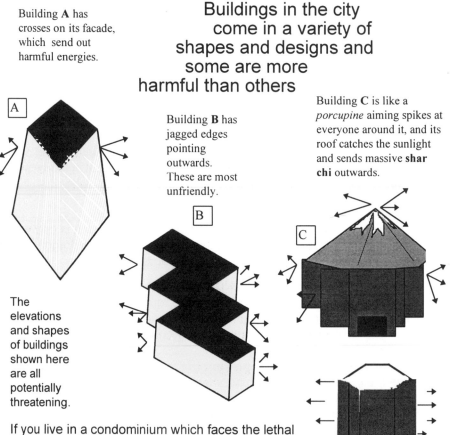

The elevations and shapes of buildings shown here are all potentially threatening.

If you live in a condominium which faces the lethal EDGES of buildings such as these, you will definitely need feng shui protection.

Hang a **Pa Kua** to directly counter the deadly negative energies shooting your way, and if you find that to be insufficiently strong, place a **miniature brass canon** outside your door and aim it at the edge.

There are 2 buildings shaped like this in Kuala Lumpur. The edges are virulent

Look out for cross shaped escalators in the lobby of the building across the road. They could harm you !

Buildings that cause feng shui problems to their neighbors eventually suffer the result of protective measures taken by others against them. When Pa Kuas or cannons are used in retaliation, these in turn send out dangerous energies. Thus knowing some basic feng shui helps you ensure that YOUR own home or any building you design do not hurt others.

THE BEST CURE against buildings that seem threatening, is to place a large **fountain** in front of the entrance into your building. This benefits everyone in your apartment block, and fountains also bring masses of pleasant and auspicious sheng chi, so it might be a good idea to get together and share the cost. Fountains also do not cause harm to your neighbors.

Also look out for angular designs or patterns which have sharp points, that are placed as decoration in buildings near you. These may serve to enhance the building across the road from you but they could well be damaging.

ANOTHER SOLUTION is to resort to the use of a **cannon,** especially if you are having to combat very powerful shar chi caused by massive structural features like triangular designs or cross shaped escalators. But cannons are extremely harmful to the party being hit, and so I really do not encourage it UNLESS you really have no other choice.

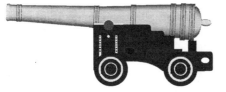

CROSSED SWORDS or a painted crest featuring crossed swords is also a powerful combative tool, but like the cannon it is a hostile approach towards solving your feng shui problem.

The roads around your house or apartment block can be either auspicious or inauspicious depending on whether they are straight or curving, and if they curve, whether they are curving around your house or curving away from your house. It also depends on whether the roads are higher or lower than your house, and whether you are being hemmed in by roads in front of or behind your house.

First see if straight roads are directly hitting at your front door

If you live directly at the end of a straight road, or your house is located smack in front of a **T** junction, the road is symbolically hitting you with a great deal of killing energy. Curved roads are can be harmful or auspicious. In the drawing on the right here, house B is more auspiciously placed in relation to the road than house A. This is because house B is being *embraced* by the road, while house A is being *hit* by the road. The same principle holds for buildings.

Next examine the junctions near your house

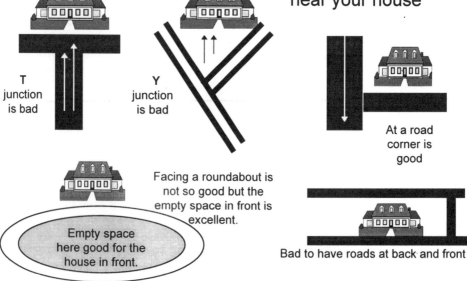

T junction is bad

Y junction is bad

At a road corner is good

Facing a roundabout is not so good but the empty space in front is excellent.

Empty space here good for the house in front.

Bad to have roads at back and front

Next, check how road levels affect your house

The least troublesome from a feng shui perspective is to have a road in front of the house and on the same level as the house. There should not be a road behind. The house shown here has good feng shui.

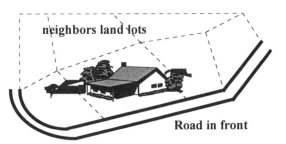

neighbors land lots

Road in front

When the road level is higher than your land, it often creates problems. Usually there is also a hill facing you, rising from the road level. This is bad feng shui. And if you build your home on stilts, it is also bad feng shui.

<u>CURES:</u> in the example shown here, it is vital to orientate the house such that its back is to the hill. This means building a driveway round to enter the house from the valley side. The important rooms should be above road level. Then make the area that is below road level into play rooms. Close up with walls.

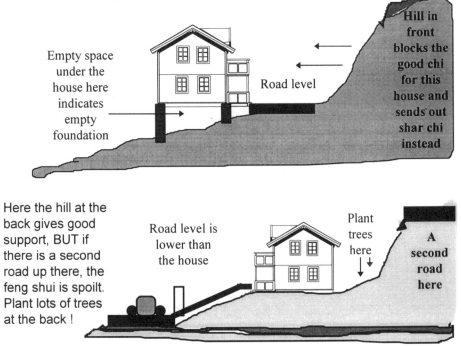

Empty space under the house here indicates empty foundation

Road level

Hill in front blocks the good chi for this house and sends out shar chi instead

Here the hill at the back gives good support, BUT if there is a second road up there, the feng shui is spoilt. Plant lots of trees at the back !

Road level is lower than the house

Plant trees here

A second road here

Speed of traffic flow and feeder roads also affect your feng shui

When the traffic flows gently, the sheng chi has a chance to gather, accumulate and settle, and when there are feeder roads with a slow flow of traffic moving pass your building, everyone living in there will benefit. If the traffic is too fast however, the chi becomes malevolent.

Two feeder roads flow into the road which passes this building

Slow moving traffic is better than fast moving traffic

Roads in cities are like rivers. When they get choked up with massive traffic jams, the effect is similar to rivers being polluted and blocked with debris. When arteries get blocked health suffers. Highways are like raging rivers which transform energies in the atmosphere into malevolent conveyors of deadly chi. Overhead roads and by-passes whose level rises above your house , or cuts into the belly of your building are terribly inauspicious. The same can be said for light transit railways. When they hug you however, as shown below, the effect is auspicious if the movement of the vehicles are not too fast.

The flyover, or light transit tracks built next to this apartment block is hugging the building. The effect is therefore not harmful.

The elevated road here cuts into this town house. The effect of this flyover is deadly and lethal, and there is little that can be done. The energies are too fierce !

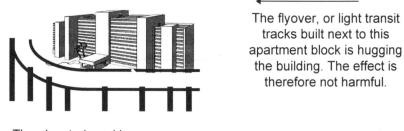

When a new house gets built next to, or opposite yours, or when a new development gets constructed in the vicinity of your apartment block, you can be sure your feng shui will be affected in some way. Or when a neighbor's small tree grows into a big tree. Or when new gates with harmful designs get installed. When you start to see your immediate surroundings with *feng shui eyes*, you can usually ignore the small things like pointed letter boxes, telephone poles and upward pointing spikes that seem to be offending your feng shui. These items may not be especially good for you, but their effect is small and can be easily dealt with. Simply plant some bushes to cut out the view.

But you should be wary of the **triangular roofline,** or massive new gates, or a threateningly looking pine tree which has grown tall and overpowering with the years. These are features which have the potential of hurting your feng shui quite seriously if they face your main door directly. Or if they happen to be on your *tiger* side, ie the right side of your home (inside looking out).

This house here has TWO potentially dangerous triangular roof lines which will send *shar chi* outwards. If your neighbor has such a house, make sure your front door is not directly facing either of the roofs.

This house is being hurt by the neighbor's **tall coconut tree** which is directly hitting at the main door. Meanwhile the two double triangle rooflines of this house is also sending out shar chi.

Designs drawn on the front of your house should be auspicious !

Look at the downward pointing arrow painted on the front of this house. Symbolically not advisable !

Roof shapes too should bring luck

The roof of your house should appear protective, like a canopy. The top portion should thus protrude upwards slightly, although the angle should not be too steep, otherwise they become *fire* roofs. Conventional roofs are said to be auspicious feng shui. Flat roofs are not. And the increasingly popular pyramid shape is more suitable for yin dwellings than for yang dwellings. **Remember the pyramids of Egypt and elsewhere were all tombs !**

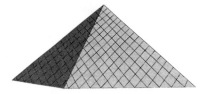

In recent years, the pyramid shape has become very popular as *caps* for multi level high rises, and I have been asked if this shape is auspicious. My answer is that I would not build my house with a pyramid roof ! Too *yin* for me !
The pyramid at the Louvre in Paris however demonstrates an excellent balance of *yin* and *yang*. It is made of glass and it brings in the light - *yang* energy into the Louvre - but only enough to attract visitors. Also remember that the museum is meant to be a very *yin* place, so the pyramid structure is ideal. Hence it has been a great success.

Conventional roof shapes are auspicious

Flat roofs are not auspicious. The house lacks a sheltering canopy.

The roof shape shown above is traditionally regarded as ideal.

Dome and round shapes are auspicious but are better suited for places of worship

84

Driveways can harm or hurt depending on several factors

Many of the grand mansions of England and the United States have a very long, and very straight approach road as shown here.

This driveway above is good for the house. It does not hit the door in any way.

Buckingham Palace in London also has the mall, a long straight road in front of it. The effect is of course bad feng shui. **BUT** if there is a rounded feature, like a landscaped garden, or a fountain between the house door and the straight road, the bad feng shui is eliminated. This CURE is also shown in the sketch above.

If the pathway (or driveway) which leads to your house widens outwards, as shown here, it is auspicious. Broad driveways are also better than narrow driveways. The driveway should not lead directly to the front door.

The driveway shown here is also auspicious as it does not hit at the main door. Allowing for some empty space in front of the main door is always good feng shui.

As a general rule, the approach to a house or building should always be subtle and friendly, not direct and threatening. Straight driveways are regarded as extremely unfriendly. The best driveways meander, or curve around the house. Circular driveways are also favorable. Landscaping with shrubs and flowering plants also bring good luck, since chi flowing pass before entering the house has a chance to collect and settle.

walls, gates, fences and boundaries

One of the best ways of safeguarding the feng shui of your private space is to make sure that your boundaries are properly delineated. The walls, fences and gates which you build around your house thus becomes significant. Although this does not afford protection against any feng shui offensive features of the larger landscape, it does serve to delineate your territory - thereby making it easy for you to practice compass feng shui, and also enable you to mark out the *dragon* and *tiger* sides of your home.

Walls are excellent for shutting out outside drains and other unpleasant features, but ...

You should also observe some of the taboos pertaining to walls that are built around your house

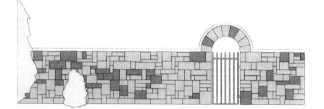

On no account should you allow your house to look like a cage or a prison. Have a solid wall behind but not on all sides of the house !

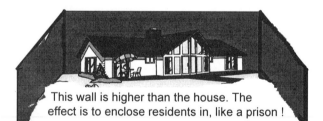

This wall is higher than the house. The effect is to enclose residents in, like a prison !

Unless you have a very large piece of land, you need to be careful that you do not end up creating an excessively *yin* area around your house. If you have trees and walls that are too close to the house itself, this is what could happen, especially if sunlight is also sparse. Indeed, it might be better to grow a low hedge with flowering plants, or have a low wall with grills on top that let the light in. This balances the yin with the yang, and can also serve to block out unpleasant sights and smells.

86

Paintings or models of your favorite wild life animals should be placed <u>outside</u> the house

When they are outside your house, placed on garage walls, or high up above the gate, the fierce spirit of these animals symbolize protection for the family. If you place them <u>inside</u> the house their ferocious spirit could be turned against you. It is the same principle as the protective Pa Kua which should always be hung outside and never inside the house. These animals can be tigers, lions, panthers, mountain goats, or eagles.

It is a great idea to place a pair of **fu dogs** on either side of the gate facing outwards to symbolize protection. In China, all the palaces and temples have these guardian fu dogs placed at the entrance.

A picture of this creature can be seen on the cover of my book The Complete Illustrated Guide to Feng shui , which is featured on the inside back cover page of this book.

A model of an eagle or peregrine, poised and alert, placed on the roof of a mansion is believed to guard the house from enemies.

PROTECTION in a feng shui context means being protected from people with dishonest or evil intentions, who will feel uncomfortable when they enter your home, as well as protection against burglars and loss.

Another great idea is to place a pair of porcelain <u>elephants </u>by either side of your main door (outside) and then place potted <u>cactus</u> plants on top of the elephants. This offers benign protection. Ceramic elephants are the specialty of Vietnam and India where beautiful models can be found. Cactus should not be placed inside the home.

Go for regular shaped land, but if you cannot, avoid triangles ..

Of course the regular shaped rectangular land plot is best, though this may not always be possible. But when buying land, do try to have land with four corners and avoid triangular shaped pieces. This is because four cornered pieces are easy to correct with lights, hedges and water features while triangular shaped land is tough to deal with. Triangular land leads to break up of marriage and family, violence and severe unhappiness.

House on triangle shaped land is most inauspicious

And orientate your house to make the best use of your land

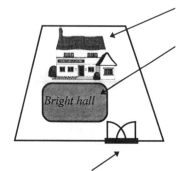

Bright hall

Position your house well back, OR at least on the **inner half** of the land.

Always try to have a space directly in front of your main door to create auspicious luck. Leave this place free of trees, pools or other tall features. Shrubs or low flowering plants are ideal. This is your **bright hall** where beneficial *chi* collects before entering your house.

Do not position your **gate** directly in line with your main door, OR with the main gate of the house opposite you.

If you have an odd shaped piece of land, divide it into regular rectangles as shown on the right here. Then identify your dragon and tiger sides. Position your house slightly nearer to the side of the dragon, and a little further away from the tiger side. Leave space in front, and place a mound of earth to raise the level of the back. Then plant trees behind to simulate the back support.

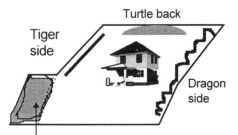

Turtle back

Tiger side

Dragon side

In the excess land, identify what direction it points to. If it lies in the North direction have a water feature like a small waterfall .. if in the South, SW or NE place a garden light, and so on ....

If you are lucky enough to have a small patch of garden, no matter how small it is, fill it with plants and flowers. Take a bit of trouble over your plants because they signify the natural growth that comes from the soil, (the earth), and feng shui is all about harnessing the luck from the earth. Once a week, get rid of dead leaves and decaying stems. What you want is the *yang* energy of healthy growing plants, and dead leaves and stems emanate *yin* energy. Choose plants that have round and wide leaves and that are easy to grow. The most auspicious plants are those that have <u>succulent leaves</u>, which suggest a store of water. The Chinese money plant is an

 excellent example. Or succulent cactus shrubs that have no thorns. Cactus with thorns grown in the garden ward off evil spirits and protect against loss, but they should never be placed indoors.

Tiger side

Dragon side

The above house shows trees at the back and on the left side of the house (inside looking out). In front, flowering shrubs would add vitality to the surrounding energy.

On the <u>tiger side</u> ie on the right side of the garden, stick to small plants and shrubs. Good to build a wall painted white on this side of your boundary.

GARDEN TIPS

If you wish to plant trees in your garden, place them on the <u>dragon side</u> and make sure they are kept under control. Do not completely block off the sunlight !

Tall <u>trees are better behind</u> the house, and never in front.

On the <u>tiger side</u> plant low shrubs. Big trees on the tiger side (or on the West of your garden) creates unnecessary strength for the white tiger.

Place red flowering plants in the South sector, blue flowers in the North, white flowers in the West and any color in the other direction sectors.

Trim your trees
and plants regularly
Trees must always be
kept under control

This tree is too tall for this house. It needs to be trimmed, otherwise it will completely block off the sun and make the house too *yin*.

This tree is definitely <u>too massive</u> to be grown in a private house garden. It will be happier in a park. Do choose your trees carefully before planting them in your garden. They may look suitable when young but as they grow, trees can become so massive as to totally overwhelm your house.

Dead stumps (above) should be completely cut down, as shown below. Otherwise the pointed branches become like poison arrows in your garden.

The bamboo

The Juniper pine

The <u>bamboo</u> and the <u>pine</u> are two excellent selections. A clump of bamboo anywhere in your garden, in front by the dragon side or at the back signifies good health and longevity for all the residents. The pine tree, of which there are many different varieties resemble an arrow pointing upwards. It thus has good symbolic meaning. The pine is also a longevity symbol, being able to withstand the most adverse conditions. Go for the blue junipers which have beautiful shape.

 # Activate the dragon in your garden by creating curved pathways

Incorporate a winding pathway onto the *dragon* side of your garden. This is the left side, (inside looking out), OR the east part of your garden. This can be a pathway of stones, or a small path that is bounded on both sides by low flowering plants

Creating a dragon on the East side of your house involves some effort especially if you want the flowers to bloom thereby signifying an active dragon. But the luck created is extremely auspicious, and so is worth the effort. Usually the natural fall of plant foliage creates a natural meandering effect. You do not require much space for this feature. The legal boundary of a ten feet width is sufficient

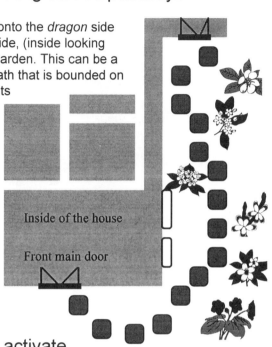

Inside of the house

Front main door

 ## You can also activate the tortoise by keeping some live ones in your garden

Keep your tortoises in the <u>North</u> part of your garden. They bring very auspicious luck !

 ## The rooster can substitute for the phoenix but do not keep birds in cages

Frogs bring good luck so if you find a toad or two in your garden, let them be ...

You can, if you wish keep a rooster as a pet in the South corner of your garden. Some of the jungle roosters of the Tropics make beautiful pets ... but on no account should you keep birds in cages in your garden (or inside your home for that matter). The Chinese believe that nothing brings worse luck than this.

Surrounding your home
with prickly plants
and weeping willows
is not a good idea

Weeping willow trees have bad symbolic connotations while an excess of prickly plants do more harm than good. Do not grow a hedge of creepers which have thorns. Not especially if the creepers are climbing on porches and garages that are too close to the house itself.

When the front of the house is flanked by two cactus plants like this however, the effect is protective.

Two tall trees like this
resembles two
joss sticks

If there are two trees like this in front of your house, flanking your entrance, the effect is most inauspicious - they resemble two joss sticks traditionally placed in front of a tomb. This chases away the *yang* energy. Far better to do away with the trees altogether.

If you place two round shaped flowering bushes however, the effect is perfectly acceptable.

Creepers are fine, but
if they completely cover
your walls, they block out
sunlight from your home

It is advisable not to let creeping plants take over the walls of your home. They could *strangle* the house, bringing ill health and illness to residents. Creepers should be used only to soften the edges of pillars and columns.

Enhance your garden with water features

You can take your pick of the vast variety of landscaped ponds, artificial waterfalls, streams, fountains and bird baths which are easily available today ... if you buy them ready made, they can be expensive. So do it yourself. All you need is a pump to recycle the water.

A friend of mine, once one of the power elite of the country had seen better days. For years he languished out of favor, forgotten ... a *has been* ... and then he discovered feng shui ...
He built an artificial stream in his garden, complete with rippling water flow caused by subtle gradations in levels - and it looks just like the sketch above. It took three years but yes, he has been rehabilitated, and today holds a very plum diplomatic posting overseas !

TIPS ON WATER FEATURES FOR THE GARDEN

- Always locate the water feature in the front half of the garden, where it can be seen from the main door. Placing water behind goes against classical feng shui guidelines.
- If possible let the water feature be on the left side of the door (inside looking out). If it is on the right side, the patriarch tends to have a roving eye and could have more than one wife.
- The best compass sectors for water are NORTH, Southeast or East, but if these directions are <u>behind</u> the house, it might be better NOT to have the water at all.
- Let your water feature be <u>round or curved in shape.</u> If it is angular, the sharp edge of a corner could be hitting at your main door.
- If you have a fishpond, design a shape which has the water embrace your house, not cut into it.
- Keep the water clean, and keep it moving. <u>Moving water</u> brings good luck. Stagnant water brings bad luck.
- If you <u>keep live fish</u>, go for carp or goldfish. If your fish die, replace them. They have absorbed your bad luck.
- Finally stay balanced. Ponds and waterfalls must be <u>proportionate</u> in size to the house. If they are too big, the water will drown you !

Enhance your garden
with outdoor lights

Place two wall bracket lights on either side of the front wall of your house. Get those with an upward pointing arrow.

Garden lights bring excellent feng shui to the home. Place them around the boundaries of your home and switch them on for at least three hours each night. Apartment blocks should definitely have lights around their boundaries.

At least make certain that you have a light in the South corner of your garden since this is the fire corner. Having a light here assures all members of your family will enjoy auspicious luck.

And **for romance and marriage luck** definitely have a light in the Southwest corner of your garden. This should help keep the flames of love alive, and enhance the marriage prospects of eligible members of the household.

Barbecue pits
should be placed in the South,
SW or NE of the garden

Decorative urns should be placed in the **earth** corners SW or NE

All the bits and pieces of things that you place in your garden should be located according to feng shui. Match the material which they are made of, or the significance of their symbolic meaning, to the element of the compass direction

Split level gardens require special attention

In the lowest part of the garden here, irrespective of directions, is the only place where you may install a water feature, or place a swimming pool, although I prefer not to unless it is the North.

The highest part of the garden should be where the back of the house is. Make sure this is the case, OR plant trees here.

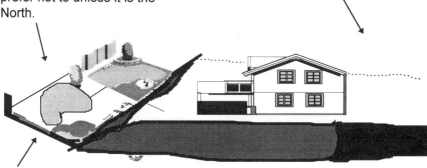

You can enhance this lowers side of your garden, since in such a configuration it is regarded as the **phoenix sector** of the garden. Plant lots of red flowers in this part of the garden - the free flowering red or bright pink *bougainvillea* planted here will bring lots of money making opportunities. Place pretty lights here to raise the *yang* energy !

1. If your house has been built on land which has a slope, check how steep the slope is. If it is too steep, you might want to have the garden terraced so that there are parts of your garden which will be level. Remember that level gardens are the easiest to deal with.

2. Never compromise on the cardinal rule of having the land behind your house higher than in front.

3. Also try to landscape the garden such that the dragon side is slightly higher than the tiger side. If this is not possible, make very sure that you plant trees on the dragon side, and low shrubs on the tiger side. This compensates for any unsuitable levels vis a vis the *dragon/tiger* configuration.

Common questions on landscape feng shui

Question: Exactly how do I determine the dragon and tiger sides of my home since this seems to be so important.
Answer: There are two methods. The first method is to stand just inside your main door and look out. The land on your left is the dragon side while the land on your right is the tiger side. The second method uses the compass directions to determine this. Thus the east side of your house or garden ie where the morning sun shines is the dragon side while the west side is the tiger side. This is the side which gets the afternoon sun. Most practicing feng shui masters use either one of these methods. It would be ideal if the left side also coincided with the East ... then you would not have to choose between the two methods. When the left side is West and the right side is East however is when problems arise. In such an instance, I would personally go with the compass direction method, although I do stress that there are feng shui experts I respect, who disagree with me.

Question: You have not said much about swimming pools. What is your feeling about these large bodies of water ?
Answer: I usually discourage the building of swimming pools in private homes. Having such a large body of water so close to the house can cause severe feng shui problems. Unless the land is very large, the danger of the pool overwhelming the house is very real indeed. It is also not easy to locate a pool correctly. If it happens to get sited on the right of the main door, for instance, the marriage of the residents get affected. And if it is located in the South, it will severely hurt the good name of the residents.

Question: What should I do if my main door is being hit by a poison arrow, and I find it impossible to reposition my door ?
Answer: You can try to tilt it slightly. Even a few degrees could make a difference. Or create some kind of barrier between your door and the offensive structure opposite - a clump of heavy foliage trees is effective, or hang a protective Pa Kua.

5 ARRANGING THE LIVING SPACE

 Interior feng shui is concerned with the arrangement of rooms, their shapes, the flow of traffic within, and with the way furniture is placed in relation to doors, windows, staircases and toilets. All of this affects the quality of the energy of the home. Interiors should thus be designed, organized and arranged to take consideration of their implications on the feng shui of one's immediate living space.

The feng shui of interiors is as important as that of the exterior environment. It is no good having excellent outside feng shui if inside, the house suffers from stagnant *chi* and residents have to endure an unbalanced flow of energy on a daily basis. Or if the energy inside is pernicious and deadly due to the presence of sharp edges all over the place. Similarly good interior feng shui is completely obliterated if the surrounding environment sends killing energy to the home from structures outside. Feng shui practice thus covers the inside and outside of the home.

We have already attended to external feng shui in the previous chapter, and we have seen that a great deal of it is based on the landscape guidelines of Form School Feng shui. For interiors, *form* school concepts continue to apply. Thus shapes and angles, structures, beams, pillars, levels and orientations of the interior living space will all be demonstrated to have feng shui implications. This and the following chapters cover significant taboos to look out for, with detailed treatment on layouts, and the arrangement of individual rooms. A later chapter deals exclusively with feng shui enhancing techniques for interiors.

The approach thus takes a **twofold perspective**, first <u>defensive</u>, ie looking out for taboos and how to correct them, thereby guarding against bad feng shui, and then, how to <u>consciously activate good feng shui</u> inside the home.

Start by determining general orientations of your home

To begin, get the feng shui orientations of your home using the diagram on the right as a guide. Draw out the layout plan, and then place a layer of transparent paper, with a nine square grid over the layout plan.

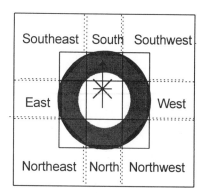

Southeast	South	Southwest
East		West
Northeast	North	Northwest

1. Once you have divided your home layout into nine squares, what you would have done is in fact to have <u>superimposed the Lo Shu square</u> onto your home. It is important that when it comes to actual demarcation of sectors (squares) the dimensions should be as accurate as possible. Also as shown in the sketch here, you must include all the covered areas of your house. Parts of the square which fall on areas that are not part of the house, indicate <u>missing sectors</u>. (see page 23)

2. Next you should invest in a good reliable compass, and take the compass orientations of your home. Do this by standing just slightly inside the main front door, and looking out, determine the direction your main door is facing. Take it from the center line of the door, three feet from the door, then once again ten feet from the door, and yet again twenty feet from the door. How you do it is shown in the sketch below.

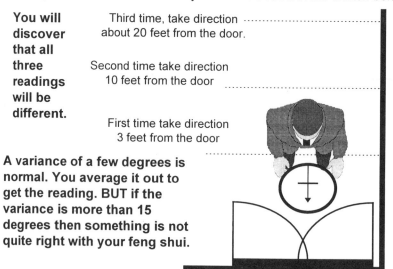

You will discover that all three readings will be different.

Third time, take direction about 20 feet from the door.

Second time take direction 10 feet from the door

First time take direction 3 feet from the door

A variance of a few degrees is normal. You average it out to get the reading. BUT if the variance is more than 15 degrees then something is not quite right with your feng shui.

Master compass feng shui experts have told me several times that when there is a variance of more than 15 degrees in the main door direction taken between three to about twenty feet apart, it is an indication that the energies of the house are seriously out of balance. This can be caused by any number of factors, either from inside the house, or from the outside.

For instance if you live too near heavy duty electricity transmission lines, the electromagnetic field affects your compass readings. Or, if inside your house, you have inadvertently placed heavy metal equipment in the wrong corner of the living room, this **A big variance in compass readings indicates that something is not quite right** too could cause the compass needle to go haywire. Proceed to investigate the *element* harmonies in the living room, make the changes and then check the reading again. Sometimes variances in compass readings could be due to nothing more than inaccurate reading. The line three feet from the door, and the line 20 feet from the door may not have been straight. At any rate, to achieve effective feng shui, readings and measurements should be as accurate as possible.

3. The next step is to mark out the <u>compass directions</u> as well as the <u>compass sectors</u> on your layout plan. Identify which is the North sector, and from there fill in the rest of the compass directions and sectors of the house.
From this exercise alone you will be able to determine the following:

- whether your house has any missing corners and if so, which are the missing corners.
- whether you have protruding corners in the home, and if so which corners they are.
- which sectors house which of the rooms, toilets and so forth
- which sector your main door is located in

Once you know the orientations of your home, you will be able to follow all the guidelines given in this and other books. You will also be able to start doing your own feng shui based on the conceptual guidelines and summarized tables of meanings given in Chapters 2 and 3 of this book. Knowing your house orientations also enable you to understand the language of feng shui with greater facility. Later, when we deal with the use and applications of Compass formulas you will also find this exercise in compass readings extremely useful.

Basic rules on layout of rooms

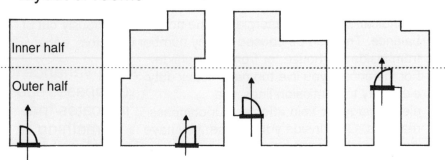

Inner half

Outer half

Irrespective of the shape of your house or apartment, the inner half and outer half of the home is determined by where the main door is located. The outer half is the <u>front part</u> of the house where you should not locate your private rooms, while the inner half is the back part of the house.

When designing your layout and allocating rooms, please note the following general guidelines:

Kitchens and bedrooms should not be located in the outer half of the home if it is a one level house. If the house has several levels, kitchens should still not be located there although bedrooms can be.

Dining rooms should preferably be located in the center of the home, neither too far to the back nor too near the front, especially the main door. If you have two dining rooms, the one used for entertaining may be located in the outer half of the home.

Allocation of sectors for each member of the family can follow the Pa Kua trigrams

If you refer to the illustrated grid on page 25, you will see the trigram associations of each of the eight compass sectors, with every member of the family. You can use these associations to guide you in the allocation of rooms.

<u>The Place of the Patriarch</u>
According to the Trigrams, the <u>Northwest</u> is the place of the patriarch. This is one corner of your home where the master bedroom or the master's study can be located. So if you were to use the NW for a guest room, a store room or the maids room, it would be a huge waste !
<u>Worse,</u> if the NW housed a toilet or the kitchen it would press down on the luck of the master of the household.

Special tips to benefit the children

Feng shui prescribes special guidelines to ensure a surfeit of good descendants luck. This is based on traditional Chinese attitudes towards the perpetuation of the family name. In this respect, sons are often given more prominence than daughters. As such <u>the East,</u> which is the place of the dragon, and which is symbolized by the growth element of wood, and hence considered most ideal for young growing children - is often allocated to the sons of the family, especially the eldest, or only son. When their bedrooms are placed in the sector East, growing sons benefit from good feng shui. They will enjoy good health and grow up strong and upright.

Feng shui recommends that daughters be given rooms in the sector Southeast, which is also of the wood element, but this is *small wood*, while the East is *big wood.*

If you have more than one daughter, or more than one son, then follow the trigram allocations on page 25.

Place your son's bedroom In the east, and your daughter's bedroom in the southeast

---

THE PLACE OF THE FAMILY
To ensure that the family stays together, and that siblings get along with each other, focus on two major rooms, the <u>family room</u> and the <u>mother's room.</u>

The family or dining room should always be in the center of the home, more into the inner half than the outer half. This ensures that the family is symbolically located in the *heart* of the house.

The best place to locate the family matriarch is the Southwest, which is also the place of mother earth. If Mum has her work or rest room here, and the corner is also properly enhanced the family benefits from what is termed
the perseverance of the mare.
The family will bloom under the wonderful care of the mother.

The importance of the West sector
When children reach their teens, the energies and *chi* flows of the West sector begins to affect them. This does not necessarily mean they need to be relocated there. However it does mean that, when children grow up, steps should be taken to enhance *yang* energy in the West sector to benefit the children. Place metal objects in the West, or hang a windchime there. And if there are trees in the West garden, cut them down !

Let the traffic flow of your layout meander

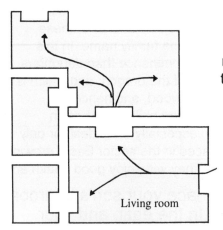

Living room

Auspicious *sheng chi* must always be given a chance to move slowly and gently through the house, and the best way of ensuring this is to design your rooms in a way which allows the traffic flow of the house to curve. Long corridors and sharp turns are strongly discouraged.

The arrangement of rooms and doorways shown on the left here allows *chi* to flow slowly and meander through the rooms. The effect is good.

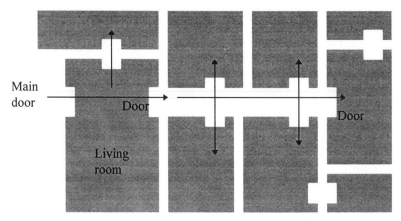

Main door

Door

Living room

Door

The sketch above shows a layout arrangement which incorporates a long corridor, along which several rooms are located. The flow of *chi* is much too fast and too strong, and it is not auspicious.
There will be lots of quarrels in this home.
The problem has been made worse by the location of the main door being in a direct straight line with two other doors within. This is traditionally a major feng shui taboo. The effect is the creation of an invisible but nevertheless lethal poison arrow caused by nothing more than the layout of the rooms and the location of the doors that link these rooms.

placement of the main door

The feng shui of the main door is probably the most crucial aspect of your overall feng shui. This is regarded as the *kou,* the mouth of your home. It is where good or bad luck *chi* enters the house.

Destroy the feng shui of anyone's main door, and you destroy his overall feng shui luck !

Thus main doors must always be protected against poison arrows, both from outside the house as well as from the inside. There are a great many taboos related to the positioning, proportion, dimensions and characteristics of main doors and it would be useful to consider them one at a time.

Main doors should <u>open inwards</u> into a <u>wide space</u> rather than a cramped, narrow corridor. Just as it is necessary to have the bright hall outside, the inside should also be relatively spacious. If there is a foyer and it is too tiny, far better to do away with the foyer.

CURES
If the door opens <u>outwards,</u> change the hinges.
When the inside foyer space is too small hang a bright light
above the door, and keep the light turned on for at least three hours
each evening. If the foyer is **dark** as well as cramped,
keep the light on 24 hours of the day !
You can also use a mirror to visually enlarge the foyer space,
but the mirror should not directly face the door.

Hang a bright light in the center of the foyer

Place a mirror as shown

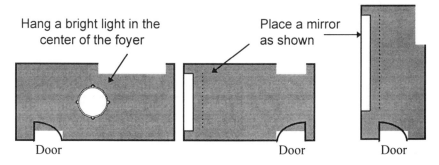

Door   Door   Door

The main door should not be too small nor too large

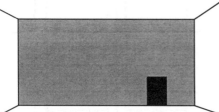

This has to do with the crucial factor of balance. The door should not be too large nor too small <u>in proportion</u> to the whole house. For apartments use the **size** and the **height** of the living room as a guide.

A door that is too small is most unfortunate. Good fortune just cannot enter into the home ! The door should be at least high enough for the tallest member of the household to walk through without too much difficulty, and it should definitely look proportionate to the room.

A door that is too large for the room will lose all their good fortune. This also means ceilings should not be too low. Wealth will be lost, and nothing can benefit.

Solid wood doors are preferable to see through glass doors

Main doors should always be <u>solid,</u> made of either wood or some other strong material. Doors must never be made of see through or opaque <u>glass</u> as this suggests fragility and is no protection for the home.

Louvre doors are also unsuitable as main doors, although they are acceptable elsewhere.

Beware of poison arrows from *inside* and *outside* the main door

<u>From the outside:</u>
Neighbor's
roof line

<u>From the outside:</u>
Edge of a building

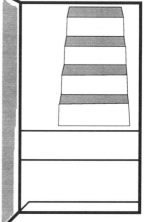

<u>From the outside:</u>
Steps leading up or down

Harmful structures <u>from the outside</u> are best dealt with by
re orientating the door so that the offending edge, pointed
angle or other harmful item no longer hits the door directly.
There are many different structures that can harm the
main door which have been dealt with in chapter 4.
The main door can also be harmed by features inside
the house and these are shown in the following sketches …

Main door greeted by a
staircase is bad

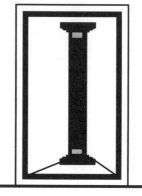

Directly facing
a column is very bad !

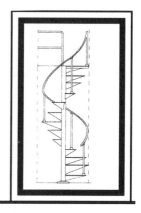

Facing a spiral
staircase is extremely bad

Mirrors do not harm the door when they are placed by the side wall next to the door. They are harmful only when directly reflecting the door.

Some more things which can hurt the front door from inside the home

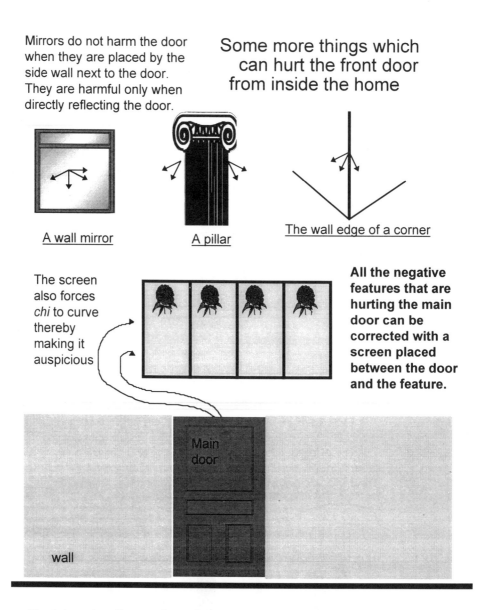

A wall mirror   A pillar   The wall edge of a corner

The screen also forces *chi* to curve thereby making it auspicious

All the negative features that are hurting the main door can be corrected with a screen placed between the door and the feature.

Main door

wall

To determine if any of the features indicated as harmful to the main door is actually hurting the door, stand outside and look in. If the feature is directly visible from the entrance just outside the door, then your feng shui is being negatively affected, and it is advisable to either remove the feature altogether, or block it off with a screen or divider of some kind.

A row of potted plants is also effective.

The main door should not face a toilet, nor another door nor a window ....

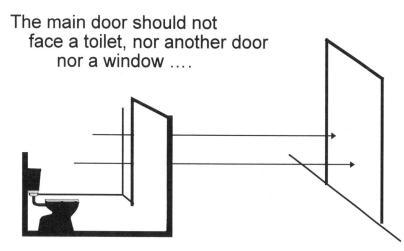

If the main door faces a toilet of the home directly, please make an effort to first keep both the toilet itself, as well as the toilet door closed at all times. Next make arrangements to try and close up the toilet door permanently by creating another door that enters the toilet from another wall. When a toilet faces the main door, it sends severe negative *chi* towards all the good energy which enters the home. This is thus a serious feature which should be attended to.

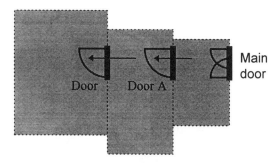

DOORS IN A STRAIGHT LINE ARE BAD

When the main door directly faces a second, and a third door, all in a row, a poisonous path of *chi* is created which adversely affects your feng shui. The solution is to relocate the inside door marked A. This transforms the straight *chi* into curving, and thus auspicious *chi.*

When there are windows directly facing the main door, any good fortune *chi* which enters the house simply flies right out again ! Windows should be placed on either walls A or B, never directly opposite.

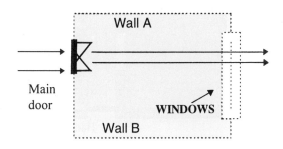

Good and bad feng shui of the main door depends on the general layout

EXAMPLE OF A GOOD FENG SHUI MAIN DOOR

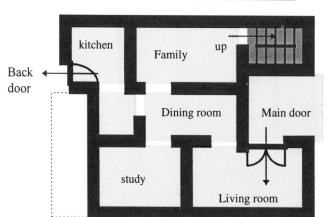

Note two auspicious features:

1. the main door is larger than the back door.
2. the main door opens to a big spacious living room.

The design of this home layout is regular and balanced. The main door location is excellent, as it forces the *chi* to curve and turn from room to room. Both sides of the main door are spacious and comfortable.

EXAMPLE OF BAD FENG SHUI MAIN DOOR

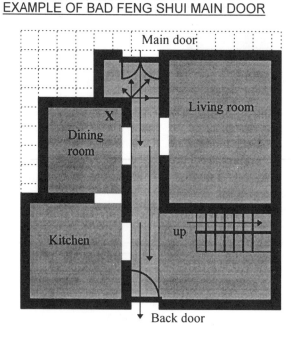

In the example shown on the left, note **two extremely harmful features**:

1. the main door forms a straight line with the back door. This is a major taboo and should be strenuously avoided.
2. There is a sharp and deadly corner pointing directly at the front door, marked X in the sketch.

Another example of a door placement requiring adjustments

Good door placements always open to some space. When the entrance is cramped either inside or outside the door, the feng shui is adversely affected. The second cardinal rule is that the main door should never be hit by any configuration, arrangement or structure which blocks the flow of traffic inwards. Here is an example of a very bad door placement I came across recently. Several adjustments had to be made to correct the feng shui.

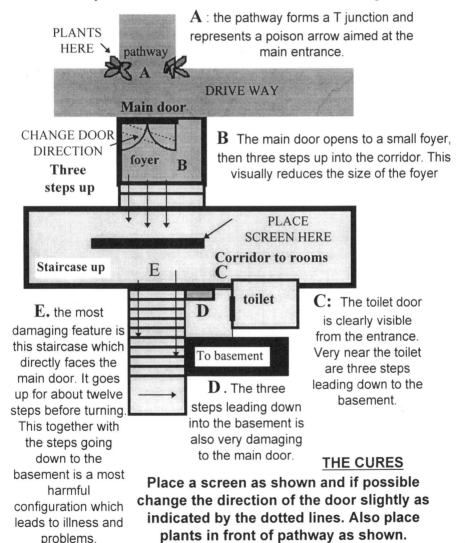

A : the pathway forms a T junction and represents a poison arrow aimed at the main entrance.

PLANTS HERE ↘ pathway

A

DRIVE WAY

Main door

CHANGE DOOR DIRECTION

Three steps up

foyer **B**

B The main door opens to a small foyer, then three steps up into the corridor. This visually reduces the size of the foyer

PLACE SCREEN HERE

Corridor to rooms

Staircase up   E   **C**

toilet

D

C: The toilet door is clearly visible from the entrance. Very near the toilet are three steps leading down to the basement.

E. the most damaging feature is this staircase which directly faces the main door. It goes up for about twelve steps before turning. This together with the steps going down to the basement is a most harmful configuration which leads to illness and problems.

To basement

D . The three steps leading down into the basement is also very damaging to the main door.

THE CURES

Place a screen as shown and if possible change the direction of the door slightly as indicated by the dotted lines. Also place plants in front of pathway as shown.

You can also enhance the feng shui of your main door

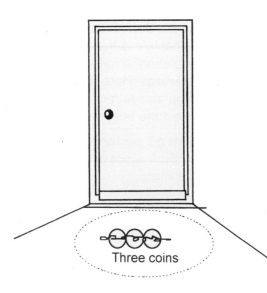

Three coins

Bury **three old coins** tied with red thread under the ground just inside the main door. If you cannot bury the coins place them on the floor and cover with a rug. This symbolizes walking on gold each time you enter or leave the home. This practice has been recommended to me by several feng shui experts, but I believe that it is more superstition than feng shui. Try it and see if it works for you.

Hang a **painting of an auspicious subject** near the door to enhance the happy energy of the front door Peonies, chrysanthemums, plum blossoms or other good fortune flowers make excellent subjects.

I have a beautiful painting of the Chinese *Sung dynasty tribute horse* hanging next to my main door on the inside. This is to symbolize plenty of presents coming into my home.

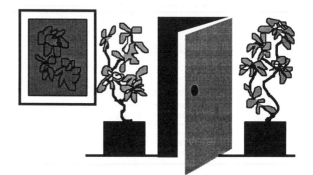

Another excellent feature is the placement of two beautiful **good fortune plants** (like the Chinese money plant) on either side of the main door. Again this raises the yang energy and attracts good fortune *chi* into the home. Remember that plants with round, broad leaves are better than plants with long pointed leaves. Prickly thorns are definitely not acceptable.

Be careful of what lies above the main door

If an upstairs toilet is inadvertently placed above the main door, it makes the entrance feng shui of the home extremely inauspicious. Even if the toilet is not directly above the door but only the entrance foyer, , the energies are still not auspicious.

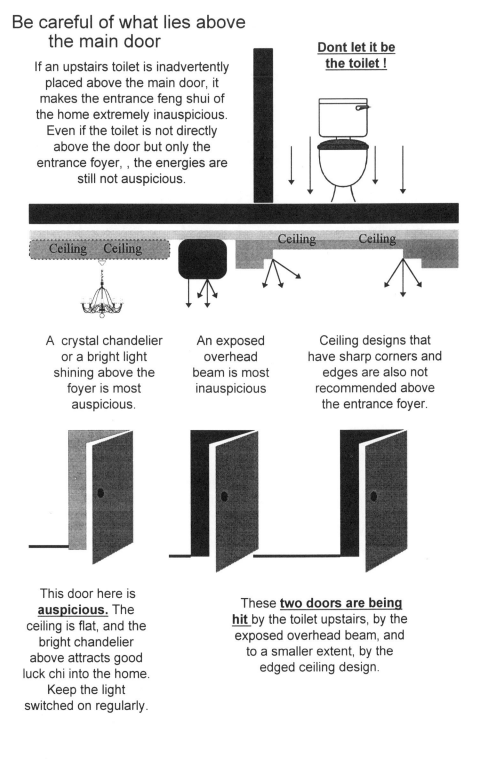

A crystal chandelier or a bright light shining above the foyer is most auspicious.

An exposed overhead beam is most inauspicious

Ceiling designs that have sharp corners and edges are also not recommended above the entrance foyer.

This door here is **auspicious.** The ceiling is flat, and the bright chandelier above attracts good luck chi into the home. Keep the light switched on regularly.

These **two doors are being hit** by the toilet upstairs, by the exposed overhead beam, and to a smaller extent, by the edged ceiling design.

Watch out for other doors and objects that are near the main door

When there are other doors near the vicinity of the main door, they create a multitude of effects, some of which can be interpreted as bad luck. We have already noted the ill effects of a toilet near the main door. In addition, main doors that face doors into bedrooms and kitchens can also cause problems, especially when the two doors are aligned in a straight line.

An arrangement like this hurts BOTH the main door as well as the person sleeping on the bed ... there will be little chance of success in such and arrangement. Another effect of this arrangement is that the people in the bedroom will become lazy and indolent .. the feng shui is certainly no conducive to success.

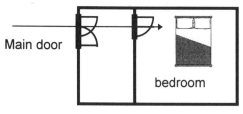

Main door

bedroom

The solution is to either move the door to the bedroom away from being in line with the main door, OR place a screen between the two doors OR hang a windchime in front of the bedroom door if it happens to be in the West or Northwest corners of the home. It is also a good idea to move the bed such that it is diagonal to the door.

and finally...
don't let your main door face...

open shelves... which act like knives cutting into your good luck

sinks and cookers which press down on your good luck

or brooms and mops ... which sweep away your good luck

Having taken care of the main door the next step in interior feng shui is to turn our attention to the other doors and windows inside the home. The first rule to remember is that doors should NOT be placed in a straight line. This transforms healthy auspicious *chi* into belligerent *chi* simply because it cause the *chi* to move too fast, and if the doors in a straight line are sandwiched by the front and back doors, the bad luck is quite enormous ... it is necessary then to create a barrier of some kind in between. It is for this reason that feng shui experts strenuously warn against three doors in a straight line. Having taken care of this, there a few other guidelines on doors that are useful to take note of ...

Main doors should not have other doors along the same wall

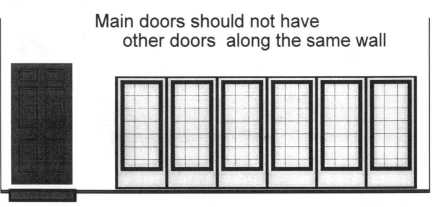

Sliding doors, French style windows that look like doors, and patio doors should NOT be aligned in a straight line with the main door.
This creates too many **mouths** in the home, leading to quarrels and disharmony.. If you have this sort of arrangement in your home, keep the secondary doors closed at all times, and hang curtains.

The main door should always be the largest door in the home. It can be the same size as the other doors, but it should never be smaller. If your main door is smaller than another door in the home, please do make an effort to correct it since this means that your ambitions will be too big for your luck to keep up with. If you want your luck to match your ambitions, make very certain that your main door does not let you down.

113

It is not a good idea
to have too many doors in a long corridor

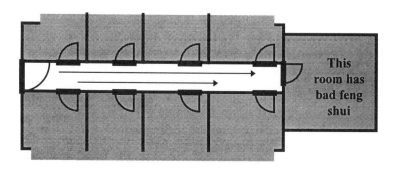

This room has bad feng shui

When there are too many doors opening off a corridor, as shown in the sketch, there will be *too many mouths* in the household ! This is interpreted to mean a great deal of bickering and quarreling. If the doors directly face each other and are equal in size and height, there is nothing wrong with the feng shui of the doors themselves. But simply having so many doors off a long corridor will create imbalance and disharmony in the household. Meanwhile, the room at the end of the corridor will suffer from bad luck and the resident here will have ill health. This is because the room is on the receiving end of the *poison arrow* created by the long and straight corridor itself.

Doors should
not be awkward ...

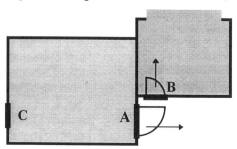

Because door A opens outwards, it clashes with the door B. **Remember that doors should always open inwards.**

Door A is also much larger than Door B. This causes the resident of Door B to be over shadowed and suffer unnecessarily from unbalanced flow of chi.

Meanwhile Door C, (which probably goes into the attached bathroom) is in a straight line with Door A. This is usually not advisable and it would be advisable to place some kind of barrier between the two doors.

As for the main door, all other doors should not directly face harmful objects

The practice of feng shui requires developing an acute awareness of the subtle energy flows within the living environment. With practice it does become second nature, and one of the rather important thing to notice is to become aware of what the doors of all the rooms in the home open into, and open out of. This means becoming sensitive to what is directly facing the door itself, and what is the first things you see each time you open the door into a room. In this context, please note that everything that is said to harm the main door, also harms the other doors within the home although the *harm* is usually limited to the occupant of the room which has the affected door. Thus toilets, staircases, the sharp edge of corners, and pillars will cause bad luck and ill health.

If any of your doors suffer from this sort of feng shui problem DO NOT HANG A PA KUA ... **hanging a Pa Kua anywhere inside the home is a terrible mistake.** The Pa Kua will hit all the residents inside the home. It can only be hung outside the house facing outwards. It should never be hung inside ... unfortunately I have come across several cases in Australia and the UK where practitioners have actually been advised to hang the Pa Kua inside the home, thereby obviously causing them immediate bad luck - a case of a little knowledge being a most dangerous thing.

Instead, try to use a curtain, a screen or some plants to soften the effects of the *bad chi* ... if it is possible to remove the offending structure or object this would be the best thing to do, but this may not always be possible. Other things not advisable from a feng shui perspective are abstract paintings with angular designs and shelves. A list of objects to look out for are shown below

Dont let your doors face any of the following ...

| Rubbish bin | Edge of Table | A television | Emblem that feature swords and guns | Pictures or paintings with cross or sharp designs |

A special word
   ## on the placement of altars

I have often been asked about the placement of altars in homes and I have to confess that I am unable to advise on the spiritual or religious side of this matter. However, to the Chinese, altars that directly face the main door, or the door into a family room are said to be acceptable, and from a feng shui perspective, this is actually quite an excellent placement. Indeed, altars that face the main door are deemed to be extremely auspicious.

Altars that directly face either the main door, or the door into the living or family room are deemed to be auspicious. But do not let the altar itself face the door into a toilet, or into the kitchen.

Similarly, do not place holy verses directly facing toilet doors or kitchen doors. This is disrespectful and creates bad feng shui. But they are excellent when placed, facing the main door.

It is also considered extremely bad feng shui to place statures of deities on the floor, or flanking a doorway since this suggests a lowering of the good positive energy which emanates from the statue deity. For those of you who are fond of antique Buddha statues for example, you would do well to observe these important guidelines. The same rule should also hold true for statues of deities of other cultures.

When you display **antiques** in your home, it is always a good idea to investigate the provenance of these antiques. Remember that *energies* (good or bad) cling on to objects, and these *energies* will affect the doorways that enter into rooms. It for this reason that I usually prefer new rather than antique furniture.

Window - to - door ratio
should not exceed three - to - one

When investigating the feng shui of the windows of your home, the first thing to note is that the ratio of windows to doors should not exceed three to one. If you have too many windows, the effect is that all the good luck chi has no chance to settle and accumulate in the home. It all flies right out the windows ! Thus **rooms should always have at least one solid wall,** and windows should not directly face the doors.

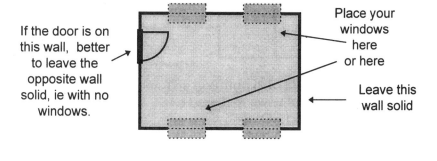

If the door is on this wall, better to leave the opposite wall solid, ie with no windows.

Place your windows here or here

Leave this wall solid

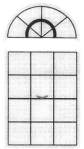

Windows which have a semi circle above, as shown here are very auspicious. The grill design however has an arrow pointing downwards, It is thus better to place a second semi circle, as shown by the solid line. This in effect changes the design of the grill and eliminates the downward pointing arrow.

Windows that open out are always preferred to windows which slide up and down. However this is only because windows which have door flaps outside *symbolically welcomes in the good luck.* So if you have windows that slide up and down it does not mean they indicate bad feng shui. It only means they are not as good as the conventional old fashioned windows.

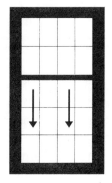

If your windows face views that suggest bad feng shui, close it off with curtains ...

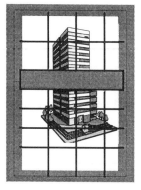

The edge of a big building is bad news !!

If a window directly faces the edge of a massive building, as shown here, the building has become a poison arrow threatening the occupant of the room. If this happens to be your bedroom window, you will find it difficult to sleep well, and could also succumb to health problems.

The best way of dealing with the unfortunate occurrence of bad feng ʹshui caused by offensive or harmful views is to block them off with heavy drape curtains. Views which cause bad feng shui are those deemed to represent poison arrows.

Do not allow trees to grow too near to windows ... Especially on the west side of the house

If your child's bedroom window opens directly to a view of a tree that is too close to the home, the feng shui of your child gets blocked. Remember that growing children need plenty of *yang* energy, and trees that are too close to the home blocks off the *yang* energy. Remedy this by trimming the tree. If there are too many trees, thin them out by cutting down a few of them.

6 ORGANIZING THE MAIN ROOMS

the main bedroom

The feng shui of the main bedroom has a huge effect on the harmony of the home, and if it is also the master bedroom of the mother and father, on the health of the marriage as well.

There are several different aspects to bedroom feng shui. Shapes are important, as are the placement of bedroom furniture and objects. The balance of yin and yang is also important, and good balance of these two cosmic forces is different for bedrooms as for other rooms. In bedrooms, the yin components which suggest calmness and quiet should, ideally prevail, because the bedroom is a place for rest, recuperation and relaxation.

The layout arrangement of your bedroom thus has important feng shui implications. But this alone does not make for good feng shui. Sleeping directions are also vital, and this implies the use of compass feng shui formulations when deciding on the exact placement of your bed.
But first some basic guidelines.

The ideal shape for bedrooms is either rectangular or square

The shape of the bedroom is often an **L** shape because of attached bathrooms. This is not so auspicious. My recommendation is to place a divider as shown, thereby transforming the bedroom into a regular rectangular shape.

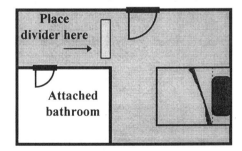

If your bedroom has an irregular shape, try to regularize it with screens or curtains strategically placed to re create a new shape for the room. But never use mirrors as a feng shui cure in the bedroom. Mirrors will do more harm than good in the bedroom.

Bedrooms should not be placed directly above the garage

When bedrooms are located above the garage or the store room, the quality of the bedroom's feng shui suffers from the lack of a base with substance. At the same time, if there are several levels in your home, the bedrooms should also Not be placed at the lowest level, and definitely not in the basement.

It is for this reason that feng shui experts generally do not like basement apartments. Sleeping underground creates an excess of yin energy, and although yin energy is conducive to sleep, too much of yin is never good feng shui.

When you sleep above the garage you will definitely be lacking in luck. Success is elusive and plans simply cannot get implemented.

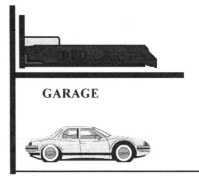

Bedrooms that are located above the kitchen suffer from intense bad luck. Sleeping on the food that is cooked for the family is bad, but having the fire below you is equally disastrous. If your bedroom is located this way, at least try to make sure your bed is not directly above the stove.

Another inauspicious feature related to the bedroom's location is when the staircase directly confronts the bedroom door. This is one of the more serious taboos of feng shui. Try to relocate the bedroom door, and if that is difficult see if you can place a screen between the top if the staircase and the bedroom door.

Much of bedroom feng shui focuses around the <u>bed</u> itself

Much of bedroom feng shui has to do with the position of the bed itself. There are feng shui implications to where it is positioned and how it is oriented. The furniture and objects that are placed around the bed also affect the feng shui of the occupant of the bed. If the feng shui of your bed is inauspicious, your marriage will be very troublesome. Misunderstandings arise over stupid and small petty things ... but bad bedroom feng shui also affects you in other areas of your life. Your mind will be unsettled and you will be lacking in concentration. This is because being hit by negative *chi* all through your sleep means you are being affected for long periods each twenty four hour cycle of the day.

Start by taking careful note of all the **bedroom taboos.** These are comprehensively listed and explained in the following pages.

But first ... a personal note from me ....
Please do not fret if you find that one or two of the taboos I describe conforms to your present bedroom - simply try to do what you can to alleviate the negative feng shui. But also remember that in feng shui, it is seldom possible to get everything right. It is the sum total of the feng shui of your entire home which in the end affects your luck, not just a few small things that are wrong. And as you grow in awareness of the chi around you, you will find that over time, you will almost sub consciously find ways and means of improving your feng shui.

It is never possible to make all the changes at once. I myself am always correcting my feng shui - as I notice things I never noticed before ... and so, over the years I have systematically improved all the corners of my room, and of my home. For instance, for a year I slept under a small overhead beam. It was funny that I never equated my headaches to that beam and then one day I saw it ... so I moved my bed away from under it ... and immediately felt better .. but in doing that I realized that now my bed was under a window !
But I also accepted the fact that it was not possible to improve things further. So I compromised and now continue to sleep with the window above my bed ... not very good feng shui but the curtain which I use to keep the window always covered does help.
So you see, if you cannot get everything right ..
it is not necessary to worry too much ...

Always try to sleep with solid support behind you …

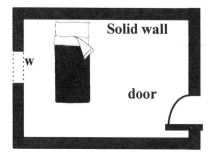

This means there should be a full length and **solid wall behind your bed**, providing you with support and a sense of security. This is an important rule to follow BUT can sometimes be compromised when you want to tap into a particularly auspicious sleeping direction that is based on compass school formula.

If your bed is positioned immediately **underneath a window,** support will be sorely lacking. It would be advisable to reposition the bed so that it is placed against a solid wall. However if you have no choice, or there are no full length walls available, then close the windows and draw the curtains when you sleep.

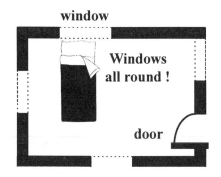

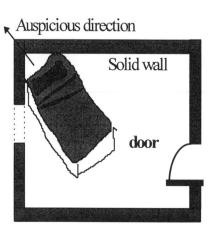

Sometimes it might be necessary to **position your bed in a diagonal way** thereby creating a triangular corner behind you … some feng shui experts say this drains energy away from the bed. However if you need to place your bed in this way in order to tap into your auspicious sleeping direction, then the benefits from tapping your auspicious direction far outweighs the corner effect. To find out what is your personal best sleeping direction please proceed to the chapter on using formula feng shui.

Bed placement in relation to the doors of the bedroom

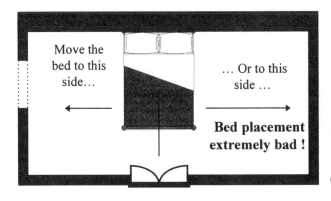

Move the bed to this side…

… Or to this side …

Bed placement extremely bad !

If the bed is placed **directly facing the bedroom door**, the effect is extremely inauspicious. This is a guideline which must NOT be compromised for whatever reason since this is deemed to be the death position.

If this door leads to an attached **bathroom and toilet,** the effect is even worse. It is very important not to place your bed this way. The best and safest way of placing the bed is thus diagonal from the entrance door ie by moving the bed either to the left or right as shown above. Be guided by the limits of what you can do with your particular bedroom.

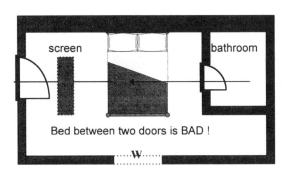

screen

bathroom

Bed between two doors is BAD !

.....W.....

If your **bed is placed between two doors**, one the entrance into the bedroom, and the other the door into the toilet, it is like a double whammy hitting at you ! This sort of placement represents very bad feng shui and you should not compromise on this rule.

In the sketch above you can see that the way the bedroom has been designed leaves little room for maneuver. Usually the solution for the two doors in a row is to place a screen as shown, and also to reposition the bed. But if you really cannot find another place for the bed then make sure you place the screen or at least some kind of divider … and always keep the toilet door closed.

Meanwhile sleeping with the feet pointed directly at the window is also not very advisable. You are placing yourself in the path of malevolent *chi.* Just move your bed a little out of the way.

Bed placement in relation to toilets and bathrooms

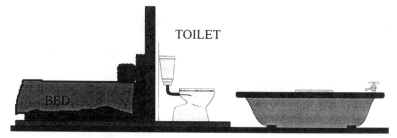

TOILET

Try not to position your bed with its headboard against a wall which has a toilet on the other side. This kind of proximity does not produce good feng shui.

Do not sleep under a toilet either ...

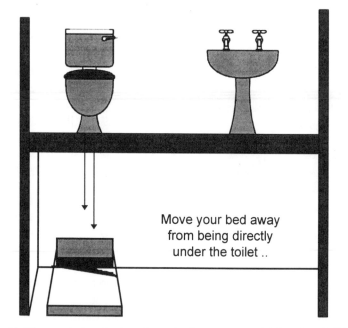

Move your bed away from being directly under the toilet ..

If your bedroom is located under a bathroom on a higher level, it is necessary to at least ensure that **the bed is not inadvertently placed directly under the toilet or WC.** The effect is similar to having water (and this case dirty water), above your head, which in feng shui indicates a situation of danger. Indeed, the presence of water too near the vicinity of the bed always spells danger and indicates the potential of loss or getting robbed or cheated.

Bed placement in relation to the presence of water features

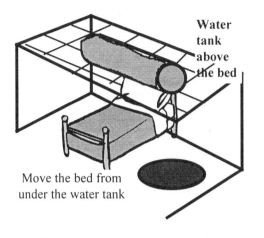

Water tank above the bed

Move the bed from under the water tank

Since you know that water above always indicates danger, make sure that you are aware where the water tank of your home is located. Do not place this tank above any of the bedrooms. If your bed does lie under the water tank, it is vital to re position the bed, as this is a very serious feng shui taboo.

Meanwhile, in your zeal to enhance your feng shui you may have been told that placing water features, like an aquarium or a small fountain brings wealth and attracts money luck. This is indeed correct, BUT water features should NEVER be placed in the bedroom. A friend of mine installed a beautiful aquarium behind her bed without telling me and promptly got held up at knife point by someone at the ATM machine and got robbed of a few thousand dollars. Here again is a case of a little knowledge being a most dangerous thing indeed.

Fish aquarium behind the bed is BAD NEWS !!

Do resist the temptation to place feng shui enhancers like fish bowls and aquariums in the bedroom. **It does not work and it could well cause you harm !**

Watch out for ...

Heavy overhead beams

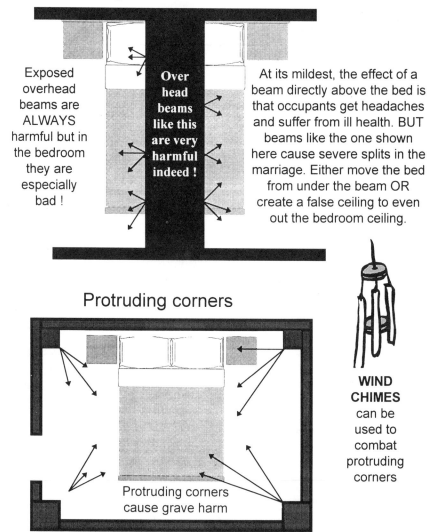

Exposed overhead beams are ALWAYS harmful but in the bedroom they are especially bad !

Over head beams like this are very harmful indeed !

At its mildest, the effect of a beam directly above the bed is that occupants get headaches and suffer from ill health. BUT beams like the one shown here cause severe splits in the marriage. Either move the bed from under the beam OR create a false ceiling to even out the bedroom ceiling.

Protruding corners

WIND CHIMES can be used to combat protruding corners

Protruding corners cause grave harm

Protruding corners also cause feng shui problems wherever they are found. Generally the shar chi caused by these corners can be easily dealt with by placing a plant in front of the corners themselves, which works by softening the sharp edge. In the bedroom however, plants should not be used, since plants in the bedroom is not good feng shui. These corners will thus have to be taken care of with windchimes that should be hung from the ceiling just in front of the corners themselves.

Fancy archways have
no place in the bedroom

I have seen the most elaborate and fancy archways built into bedrooms, ostensibly to separate the dressing area from the bedroom itself. Often I discover that these archways are directly facing the conjugal bed, and of course I am not surprised that the couple, often wealthy and affluent, decide to split shortly after moving into their multi million dollar new mansion which contains these ridiculous features ! Such archways, especially when they have triangular tops like those shown here, represent the most deadly of poison arrows. If you have features like these in your bedroom, I strenuously advice that you round up the top and place a curtain over the archway itself.

And do beware of mirrors
that face, or reflect the bed

MIRRORS in the bedroom are very very harmful to any marriage or relationship.

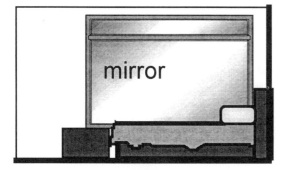

This is especially so when the mirrors directly reflect the bed, either in front of, from the sides, or even from above. It is vital to close these types of mirrors immediately if you want to save the marriage.

If you have dressing tables in your bedroom, try to place them such that the mirrors do not reflect the bed, or better still, place your dressing table elsewhere. Mirrors placed INSIDE cupboards are not harmful. But throw out mirror tiles and other fancy mirrors - they truly are completely taboo in the bedroom !

Yin and yang
energies in the bedroom

Yin and yang balance in bedrooms must reflect the nature of room usage. In the bedroom, the attributes of yin energies should prevail because this is a room of rest and relaxation. Yin is important for bedrooms and thus, there should not be too much noise level; color schemes should not have an excess of red and spotlights should be avoided. Lighting in the bedroom should be subdued, color schemes should be serene and pastel ... suggestive of calmness and quiet. There should not be a TV set in the bedroom, and elaborate music systems are not encouraged.

Having said all that however, the bedroom should not be so yin to the extent that yang is totally absent. Never forget the basic premise of the yin yang cosmology - one gives existence to the other. Thus there should also be some elements of yang energy, otherwise your bedroom will resemble a tomb ! Use your judgment and common sense when you take a overview of the feng shui of your bedroom. Have a red bedsheet if you find that you are feeling lethargic. Introduce some soft music if that is what you want - just do not go overboard and decorate your bedroom the way you would decorate your living room.

Lampshades are better than spotlights in the bedroom

Televisions in the bedroom are not a good idea. When turned on they create an excess of yang energy. When turned off they are like mirrors facing the bed. Either way TV screens represent inauspicious feng shui.

Small radios are to be preferred to elaborate stereo systems.

Using symbols of love to enhance conjugal bliss in the bedroom

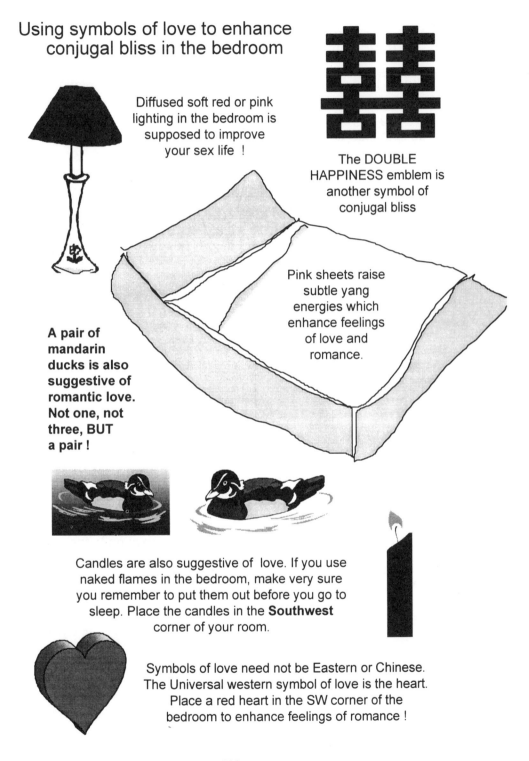

Diffused soft red or pink lighting in the bedroom is supposed to improve your sex life !

The DOUBLE HAPPINESS emblem is another symbol of conjugal bliss

Pink sheets raise subtle yang energies which enhance feelings of love and romance.

A pair of mandarin ducks is also suggestive of romantic love. Not one, not three, BUT a pair !

Candles are also suggestive of love. If you use naked flames in the bedroom, make very sure you remember to put them out before you go to sleep. Place the candles in the **Southwest** corner of your room.

Symbols of love need not be Eastern or Chinese. The Universal western symbol of love is the heart. Place a red heart in the SW corner of the bedroom to enhance feelings of romance !

If possible, tap one of your personal
auspicious sleeping directions

Bedroom feng shui should always observe the taboos relating to orientations, views, structures and shapes dealt with in the preceding pages. After observing those guidelines, the next thing to do is to *then* try to **sleep with your head pointed towards one of your four personal auspicious directions**. You can work out your personal auspicious directions by referring to the section on Compass formula feng shui contained in a later chapter. Where possible try NOT to break any of the guidelines while tapping your auspicious directions. If you find you really cannot sleep according to at least one of your four good directions, *then it is better to stick with the guidelines,* and compromise on the directions.

Here are some acceptable and non acceptable ways of tapping your sleeping directions. The arrows indicate the sleeping direction.

Acceptable (beds are well sited vis a vis the entrance door)

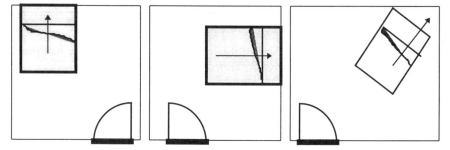

Not acceptable (beds are badly oriented in relation to the door)

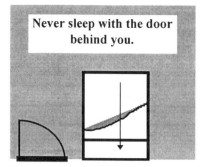

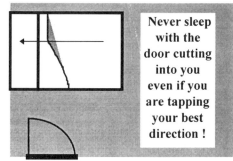

Take note of bed designs
and bed dimensions

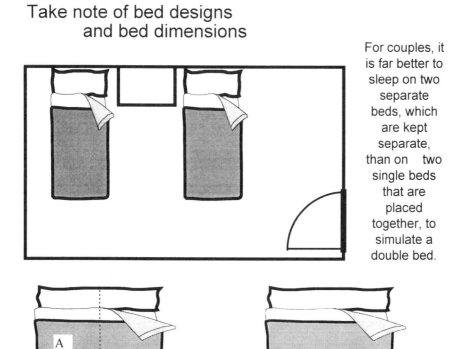

For couples, it is far better to sleep on two separate beds, which are kept separate, than on two single beds that are placed together, to simulate a double bed.

It is also important to ensure that your double bed has a double size mattress rather than be made up of two single mattresses. The split in the center (shown in A) often cause differences which could lead to a permanent split of the couple.

Also take note of **bed dimensions**. Use the *feng shui ruler* to determine that the length, breadth and height of your bed has auspicious dimensions.

Also make sure that **headboards** do not have angular or sharp edged prints that can cause problems in the night. It is always preferable to have plain colors for headboards.

Canopies above the bed are acceptable as long as they completely cover the entire bed. Canopies which end halfway down the length of the bed tend to have the same effect as an overhead beam above the bed.

Be careful when correcting
bedroom feng shui imperfections

In the bedroom, you should <u>refrain</u> from using mirrors, plants, or water to correct feng shui problems. Mirrors create unbalanced sleeping *chi.* Plants tend to be too *yang,* and water is simply unacceptable in the bedroom. The best method of correcting bedroom feng shui imperfections are screens and furniture.

Screens
Place a screen between the bed and the door if the door is directly in front of or behind the bed. Use a screen also to correct inauspicious **U** or **L** shaped bedrooms.

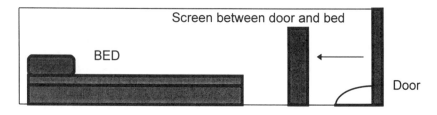

Furniture
This is probably the best method of correcting inauspicious and irregular bedroom shapes, sloping ceilings and bedrooms which have too many corners.

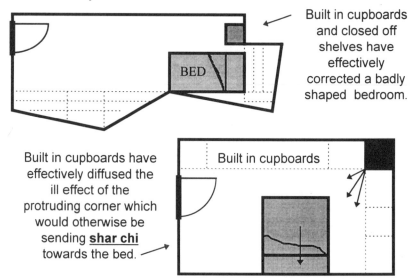

Built in cupboards and closed off shelves have effectively corrected a badly shaped bedroom.

Built in cupboards have effectively diffused the ill effect of the protruding corner which would otherwise be sending **shar chi** towards the bed.

Other bedrooms

Depending on whether they are occupied by the children or by the elderly members of the family, there are ways to plan the other bedrooms in a home to create maximum feng shui benefits. Generally speaking, children's bedrooms are better located in the East during their early childhood years, and then moved to the West as they grow into adulthood. Older members of the family should preferably be placed in the West of the home.

These however, are general guidelines only. Based on compass feng shui, the allocation of bedrooms can also be determined according to the personal auspicious directions of individuals and these are worked out according to dates of birth and gender of the child.

In addition, one can also *allocate bedrooms according to the Pa Kua's trigrams* placed around the eight directions in the Later Heaven arrangement. Please refer to page 25 for the table which summarizes this.

Generally also, the main taboos already dealt with for the main bedroom also apply equally to the other bedrooms of the home, particularly those that address shapes, harmful *poison arrows* and structural orientations that cause feng shui problems. Some additional examples of the latter are summarized here.

Bedroom Doors

- should NOT directly face a staircase
- should NOT directly face a stand alone pillar
- should NOT directly face any sharp edge.
- should NOT directly face a protruding corner
- should NOT directly face a toilet
- should NOT directly face the main front door
- should NOT directly face the back door
- should NOT directly face a stove or cooker
- should NOT directly face a refrigerator
- should NOT directly face any sharp object.
- should NOT directly face the bed itself.

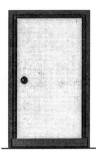

Children's bedrooms should be more *yang* than *yin* but beware of negative energy !

Because they are growing and are supposed to be full of energy, feng shui experts always recommend that young children's bedrooms should have more *yang* than *yin* features. This means more light, more noise, brighter and generally more *alive* in terms of color and energy levels. Thus if your child pins posters of pop idols, plays loud music, has the TV or radio blaring through the day - it all spells good feng shui ! Not only will health and energy levels generally be strong and vigorous but their share of good luck is also simultaneously enhanced.

But *yang* components should not be energized to the extent that there is a complete deficiency of *yin* energy ie a total absence of quiet, rest, solitude, and dark, hushed colors.

Let there be light but not so much as to altogether smother the need for rest and rejuvenation. And let the pictures around the wall be friendly rather than hostile !
Thus:
a lovable dolphin, usually associated with happiness, fun and joyousness symbolizes better feng shui than a fierce looking, hostile and unfriendly alligator.

Symbols of war and fighting - like tanks, war ships and fighter jets - while they make good toys, will generate a great deal of negative energy in a child's bedroom thereby impeding the flow of the harmonious energy so necessary for a good night's sleep. Keep such toys stored away !

Note placement of study desks in your children's bedroom

Not many parents realize that the feng shui of their child's bedroom, and in particular the placement of the child's **bed** and **desk** can often play havoc with the *child's health*, his or her *performance at school* as well as on the child's *general behavior.*

If you want your children to have good feng shui, first observe all the rules of bedroom feng shui. Next, make certain that the bed location and the child's sleeping direction, do not break any of the major guidelines. If the child can sleep with his/her head pointed to the most auspicious personal direction, so much the better.

Next take note of the placement of the study desk in the bedroom. Here are a few worthwhile tips to observe:

Position the desk so that your child can sit facing his or her most auspicious direction. This creates excellent exam luck as well.

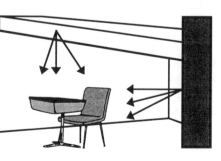

Do not place desk with a window or a door behind the chair.

Do not have a tree growing too near to your child's bedroom.

Dont get hit by a protruding air conditioner or an exposed overhead beam on top of the desk. The *shar chi* creates bad luck

Also don't get hit by the sharp edge of any cupboard, pillar or protruding corner nearby.

135

Examples of good and bad furniture arrangement in a student's bedroom

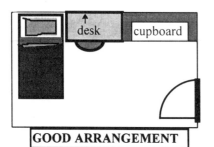

GOOD ARRANGEMENT

GOOD ARRANGEMENT

GOOD ARRANGEMENT

Try to observe basic feng shui guidelines when arranging the furniture in a student's bedroom. Focus on the bed (sleeping direction), and the desk (working and studying direction). Never sleep or work with the entrance door behind you.

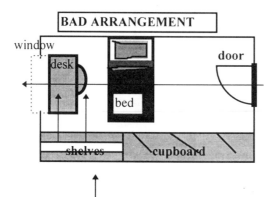

BAD ARRANGEMENT

The open shelves are sending out knives to the person sitting at the desk. Build some doors to close up the shelves.

This is a very bad arrangement.

Several things are wrong...

- the door and the window in a straight line is bad ...
- The bed between the door and the window is bad...
- The desk between the door and the window is also bad...

Never sit with your back to the door if you can help it. The rule of thumb is to keep the door within view.

Energizing the education corner
of your child's bedroom

There are several methods to create really good study and examination luck in your child's bedroom, and these methods have to do with activating the correct corners of the bedroom. The first method is universally applicable to everyone. This involves creating auspicious and good energy for the **NORTHEAST** corner of the bedroom. This corner is represented by the trigram *KEN* which is symbolic of a mountain, a time of preparation. The meaning of *KEN* is that there is a huge store of good things hidden in the mountain, and with correct preparation, these goodies can be brought forth !

The trigram KEN

If there is a toilet in the NE corner of the child's bedroom, it might be an excellent idea to find him/her another room during the growing up years. Otherwise place a big rock in the attached bathroom to symbolically press down on the bad luck thus created.

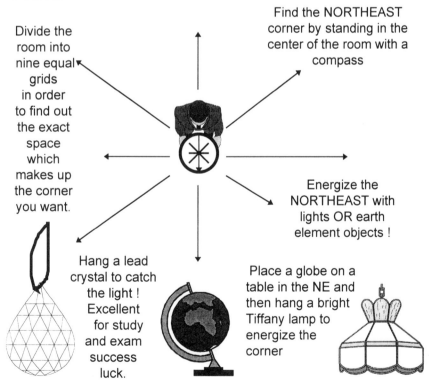

Divide the room into nine equal grids in order to find out the exact space which makes up the corner you want.

Find the NORTHEAST corner by standing in the center of the room with a compass

Energize the NORTHEAST with lights OR earth element objects !

Hang a lead crystal to catch the light ! Excellent for study and exam success luck.

Place a globe on a table in the NE and then hang a bright Tiffany lamp to energize the corner

Check your son or daughter's *success directions* and then activate accordingly

If you turn to the chapter which deals with advanced compass school formulas you will be able to determine the success directions of your son or daughter based on the date of birth and the gender. Once you know what his/her personal success direction is, you should incorporate it into the feng shui of his/her room. I have written an entire book on this formula simply because the use of this formula is extremely breathtaking in its scope and usage. In **basic feng shui** however all you need do is ensure that you sleep, work and study while facing your success direction ! At the same time you can also energize the success corner by incorporating the *theory of the five elements* in your practice. Thus for instance if your success direction is EAST, then you should energize the East corner of your room with the wood element, which is the element of the East. However, because we are dealing here with the bedroom, it is not very advisable to put plants in the East corner of the room. Much better to simply use wooden paneling, wood furniture or incorporate the color green or brown into the decor of the East corner ... Here are my suggestions for energizing the various corners of the bedroom.

 Energize the **EAST** corner with a small porcelain or wood carving of the dragon. Or use objects that are made of wood. The same can also be done for the **SOUTHEAST**

Energize the **NORTH** with a picture of the turtle or tortoise rather than use the water element. Remember that water in the bedroom cause loss and burglary.

 Use **rosettes** with different colored ribbons to symbolize success. Use red for **SOUTH, SW,** and **NE.** Use ochre or earth hues for **SW** or **NE**; use green for **EAST** or **SE**; Use blue for **NORTH** and use gold or silver for **WEST** or **NW** .

Place all your metallic trophies in the metal corners ie in the **WEST** and the **NORTHWEST.** This is particularly beneficial for West group people.

... and watch out for secret
poison arrows in the bedroom

For some months I wondered why my nephew seemed to be having such a hard time achieving even small improvements in the grades he was getting. I had given him very specific instructions on how he should sleep, how he should sit while studying and doing his homework, how he should arrange his bedroom, and even which bedroom in the house he should use. I was such a nag and so insistent that I am certain he carried out my instructions to the letter ! And yet, although he seemed to work really hard, he was simply getting no where in terms of actual, tangible achievement. His grades stayed dismally disappointing. And then one day, I found myself driving to visit him unexpectedly, and upon entering his room, these were the *poison arrows* I discovered in his room ! Let me share my findings and what I did with you, so the same thing does not happen in your children's work area.

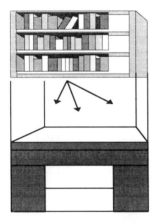

Book shelves directly above the desk, or nails, or hooks all represent poison arrows !

nails

My nephew had a book shelf directly above his desk, with the edge of the shelf directly hitting his forehead ! And as if that was not bad enough, he had also placed a few nails onto the edge of the shelf (to hang things, he told me sheepishly !) ...he was not to know that the shelf and the nails represented secret poison arrows ! *We took down the book shelf immediately, and the nails went with the shelf.*
My nephew's grades took a quantum leap in improvement after the feng shui corrections were made.

the living room

In feng shui it is useful to appreciate the subtle differences of energy patterns in living rooms and family rooms. My definition of the living room is that it is the room where I entertain guests and visitors to my home. For purposes of feng shui the way you organize your living room must depend on your lifestyle. Thus if you entertain fairly often at home, then your living room becomes an active high energy area, which can be harnessed to create plenty of yang energy for the rest of the home. generally living rooms should be fairly large in relation to the rest of the home, regular in shape - either square or rectangular and located in the outer half of the home. let the main door open directly onto the living room. If a small foyer separates the living room from the main door, then make sure the foyer is well lighted.

Shown below is a formal living room which is well balanced and has several good feng shui features.
Sofa arrangement excellent. French windows wide and welcoming.
Plants and lights give good yin and yang balance.

Archways in the living room
are excellent conveyors of chi

Whether they are curved or rectangular in shape, big archways in the living room are excellent because they encourage the gentle flow of chi within the home. Shown on this page are two examples of archways which have been cleverly incorporated into the interior design of living rooms.

The picture on top shows a **curved** archway, while the bottom picture uses design features to dress up an **angular** archway. Both pictures show good living room feng shui.

Use mirrors in the living room but watch what they reflect !

A very common living room design feature that is extremely popular in places like the UK and the USA, especially in apartments, is the use of a decorative mirror placed above a fire place as shown in the two pictures on this page. The combination of the mirror with the fireplace does not have any feng shui connotation, either good or bad. The effect of the mirror on feng shui depends on what it is reflecting. If it directly reflects the main door, or a toilet door, or the staircase, it is not auspicious. In the pictures below, the mirrors complement the room's feng shui by creating a feeling of space and this is excellent feng shui.

The living room is the best room to create _enhancing_ feng shui features

If you look again at the pictures on the opposite page you will notice several decorative features - _plants, paintings, flowers, ceramic urns, lamp shades and yes, mirrors_ ... all these items can be placed in a way that can actually enhance the feng shui of your home. The important thing is to know how to place these items in any room, and where to locate them. There are different ways of
arriving at a method but I have found that the easiest and probably also the most effective way is to apply the theory of the five elements according to their associations with each of the corners of the Pa Kua. Start by visually dividing your living room into nine equal grids to demarcate the eight corners of the room. Then use the objects according to the elements suggested by the items. Two examples are summarized below:

Place **plants and flowers (** wood element) in the wood sectors of the room. this will be the EAST and the SOUTHEAST. Also, since wood produces fire, plants can also be placed in the SOUTH to enhance the fire sector.

Place **decorative ceramics** - pottery, artistic urns, aesthetic vases (earth element) in the earth sectors of the room ie the SOUTHWEST and NORTHEAST, and also in the center. And since fire earth produces metal, they can also be placed in the WEST and NORTHWEST to enhance the metal sectors.

 If you hang **paintings** in the livi room, remember th landscapes that

incorporate lakes, rivers and mountains are generally better feng shui than abstract art. Use your own sound judgment. Paintings that show scenes suggestive of ugliness, old and tired people, or abstractions of poverty cannot possibly be good feng shui. Use instead paintings that incorporate happiness, ,joy and laughter.
Do avoid paintings that indicate tears and unhappiness.
Place paintings of mountains on the NORTH, or the EAST walls.
Water scenes are also suitable in the NORTH.
Portrait paintings of family patriarchs are best in the NORTHWEST.

Enhance the Southeast corner with
a well lighted and bubbling aquarium

Probably one of the best features to have in the living room, and especially in the SOUTHEAST, is a bubbling aquarium filled with good fortune fish like the Carp, the Arrowana or stunning Goldfish. If you are keeping goldfish or carp keep eight gold/red colored and one black specimen. If you are lucky enough to find yourself the Arrowana (a tropical river fish, which costs a great deal of money, and generally associated with wealth), one is quite sufficient, and do not place any decorative weeds or stones. The Arrowana loves living in splendid isolation !

Do maintain a sense of balance. Make sure the size of the fish tank blends in with the rest of the room. The SOUTHEAST represents wealth and placing a water feature in this corner, or along the wall enhances the income of residents. If you find it impossible to create this feng shui energizer because your entrance happens to be exactly placed in the SE, then the next best thing is to place the fish aquarium alongside the NORTH wall. The effect of this will be to give your career a real boost. Other suitable water features are a painting with water or a miniature fountain with water constantly flowing.
The movement of water in the living room creates wonderful and auspicious yang energy.

Water fountains
in the living room are great feng shui
energizers BUT do not place these
features in the bedroom.

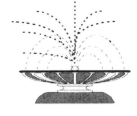

At the same time, do not forget to disarm *poison arrows* around the room

Protruding corners
Use a leafy plant to camouflage sharp corners like the one shown above. Also move the sofa from below the terrible poison arrow created by the sloping ceiling.

Overhead Beams
Everyone sitting underneath these exposed overhead beams will suffer from perpetual headaches.

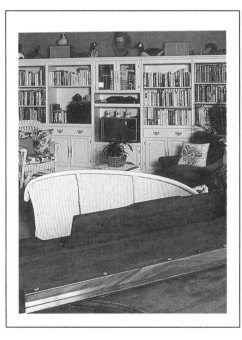

Open Book shelves
It is never advisable to have open and exposed book shelves in the living room. The rule also holds true for offices and study rooms.

This is because the shelves act like *knives* that cut into residents of the room. The shelves shown in this picture should be closed with doors.

Window views from the living room
should be shut out when harmful, and
reflected in with <u>mirrors</u> when auspicious.

Look at the view seen from this window. Usually a building like this would be considered inauspicious, and should be shut out of sight... in this case however, the tall building is too far away to do much harm.
Plus the urn of flowers near the window creates protection from any *shar chi* which may be created.

A view of flowering shrubs or plants, OR a well landscaped garden is always excellent feng shui if they can be reflected into the living room.

Patio gardens and window boxes are excellent feng shui if located in the Southeast ...

Remember that the Southeast always represents wealth luck, and because it is also of the wood element, having a luscious growth of plants in the SE always spells good prosperity luck. This wood type feature is also auspicious in the East and in the South.

If you live in an apartment on the upper floors and do not have a garden, use window boxes filled with flowers to create precious *yang* energy. Another method is to see if you can decorate lavishly with beautiful plants and indoor trees, as shown in the picture above. This indoor garden effect is especially auspicious in a room with a SE or East orientation.

Arrangement of furniture, and colors used, should demonstrate *yin yang* balance and *element* harmony

Not just in the living room but also in family and dining rooms, there should be sensitivity to a proper balancing of *yin* and *yang* energies. This is done by ensuring that rooms do not get too cold (excessive yin) nor too hot (excessive yang). Colors should be warm and welcoming but not hot ! Check the attributes of *yin* and *yang* on page 48 and you will understand how to balance these two cosmological forces. When doing this pay attention to color schemes and combinations. Let the colors of your walls, your curtains, your carpets and your sofas reflect this balance.

In addition also take note of the need for element harmony. Thus you will recall that each corner of the room corresponds to one of the five elements, so make sure your choice of colors and placement of furniture does not result in obvious clash of elements.

Example: if you have a **fireplace,** try not to have it placed along the North wall/sector of the living room. The fireplace is ideally placed in the South ! This is because the south is the place of the fire element. But of course you also know that fire produces earth so having the fireplace in the earth corners is also good feng shui. The earth sectors are Southwest and Northeast.

Element harmony can also be achieved in the use of shapes. The element associations with shapes are as follows:

The SQUARE represents the earth element

The ROUND shape belongs to the metal element

The TRIANGLE shape belongs to the fire element

The **rectangular** shape belongs to the wood element

The WAVY shape belongs to the water element

If you have split levels in your home, let the lower level be the living room

Since the living room is the place where you entertain guests, it does not matter if in terms of floor levels, it lies below the other rooms. Thus it is better if, for example the dining room, the study or the bedrooms are on higher levels.

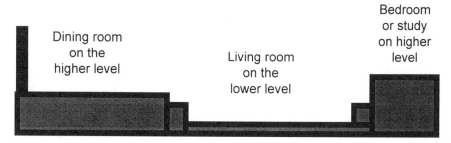

Dining room on the higher level

Living room on the lower level

Bedroom or study on higher level

Best arrangement of furniture is to simulate the Pa Kua shape

In the living room, the best arrangement of furniture is to have the coffee table in the center, and to place the sofas around the table in a way which suggests the Pa Kua. This means sofas and chairs are placed round the main coffee table and side tables are then placed between the sofa and chairs in a diagonal arrangement as shown below.

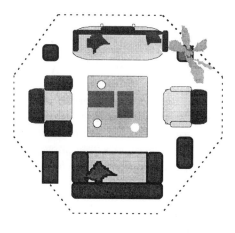

There can be variations in the way the furniture gets placed around the coffee table. But let the overall shape created resemble a Pa Kua.

Avoid furniture arrangements which are **L** shaped or **U** shaped since these are inauspicious.

The dining room

The ideal location for the dining room is the **center** or near the center of the home. When the *heart of the home* is regularly occupied by the whole family, it creates a great deal of harmony for the household. This is demonstrated in the sketch below which shows the overall layout of the house with the dining room highlighted. Then each member of the family should sit facing their respective auspicious directions.

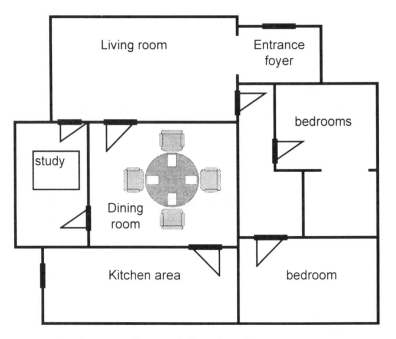

Each member of the family can select personalized auspicious direction.

The way to capture personal auspicious directions is to sit and eat facing your luckiest direction based on the formula given in a later section of this book. According to the formula every person has four auspicious and four inauspicious directions that is based on the year of birth and gender.

The ideal dining room is symbolically, always laden with food

<u>Here is a dining table which has excellent feng shui.</u>

1. It has a good **shape (** rectangular with rounded edges)
2. The **table is filled** with luscious fruits at all times.
3. The **lighting** is auspicious being in the center above the table.
4. The **mirror** reflecting the dining symbolizes a doubling of food on the table and is thus excellent feng shui.

Auspicious shapes for dining tables are round, oval and rectangle.

Round shaped dining tables represent the metal element and are ideal in dining rooms located in the West and Northwest.

Long or rectangular shaped dining tables represent the wood element and are ideal for dining rooms located in the East and Southeast.

In the example shown here, note also that the dining table is located next to the living room on the left and the kitchen on the right. This is obviously a small apartment. In such cases, **make sure that the dining table is not within view of the main entrance door**.
If it is, the feng shui is much better if a **screen** is placed between the sofa and the dining table. This symbolically separates the dining and kitchen area from the front of the home.

The steel pillar in the center of the room has a very negative effect on an otherwise lucky dining table. The feng shui would improve if the pillar was wrapped round with a creeping plant.

152

Paintings hung in the dining room
can have important feng shui implications

PAINTINGS
in the dining room should be chosen with care. Pastoral scenes are fine but not great. Pictures of ancestors emit excessive *yin* energy. The best subjects are food and fruits !

Having a **clock** in the dining area is considered bad feng shui because clocks suggest the passage of time, and this clashes with the symbolism of food and eating ! Certainly they should not be placed in front of a mirror as the bad effect is also symbolically doubled.

Dining rooms should always suggest growth and health, and *yang* energy is far more important than *yin* energy. Thus the dining room should be bright, well lit and would also benefit from a TV or radio to create some noise level. Never place the dining table underneath a beam, or worse still have the dining room itself located under a toilet on the next level.

Where the family eats - in the living room, the kitchen, or the garden affects the feng shui

If the family dines in the living room in full view of the main door, it will be difficult for the family to save money.

Occasional dining outdoors is fine but when a family always dine in the garden without a roof above, the family will lack support and shelter. The feng shui is thus negatively affected.

Dining in a sparsely furnished room can be excessively *yin*, especially if the table itself has a glass top, and the door has glass panes. The room will benefit from some *yang* features.

If the kitchen also doubles up as the dining room, as shown here, the effect is the symbolic extension of the kitchen which is not necessarily a good thing. Some kind of barrier (like a screen) should be placed between the cooking and the eating areas.

Eating while seated under exposed beans as shown here, distracts the mind and cause chi to become unbalanced. Health and appetites suffer as a result. Conceal the beams with a false ceiling or creeper plants.

Enhance the feng shui of your
dining room with *Fuk Luk Sau*

The Chinese strongly believe that if you place the Three Star Gods, what they refer to as *Fuk Luk Sau* - the Gods of Health Wealth and Prosperity - in a place of prominence in your dining room, they will symbolize great good fortune for the household. These Star Gods are rarely worshipped at an altar. They are regarded more as symbolic representations than as deities, and thus have little religious significance.

Fuk Luk Sau
is present in most Chinese homes in Hong Kong, Taiwan, Malaysia and Singapore. They symbolize abundance, long life and wealth for the household, and are easy to find in Chinese supermarkets. They are made in all sizes and you can get them in ceramics, as wooden sculptures, as cloisonné ware or simply as paintings or painted onto decorative urns.
Do remember that they are not worshipped or prayed to as deities. But do treat them with respect ie do not place them on the floor.

Another enhancing technique for the dining room is the placement of **paintings of abundant food and fruits**. There are some magnificent copies/prints of oil paintings by the old Masters which feature luscious fruits, and these are wonderful feng shui enhancers for the dining room. It is also a good idea to place ceramics that are related to *longevity* symbols, especially **peaches** in the dining room. Finally, if possible do try not to have any toilets located adjacent to the dining table. If there are toilets around, remember to keep toilet doors closed at all times.

7 KITCHENS, TOILETS & STORE ROOMS

The main thing to remember about the kitchen is that this should always be located in the **inner half** of the home, and preferably pressing down on one of your personal **inauspicious** locations.

Kitchens are not places in the home where you can do much enhancing luck. Kitchens are meant to be places where all the bad luck of the household gets burned away by the symbolic cooking *fire* of the kitchen. In terms of good luck, the appliances which have a role to play in terms of enhancing this luck are the kettle and the cooking appliances. This can be the rice cooker in Oriental kitchens or the oven in western kitchens. Make sure the kettle and the cooking appliances - are getting their source of energy ie the gas or electricity from a direction that is auspicious for you. Thus if your auspicious direction is East, then the source of gas or electricity must enter the appliance from the East direction. This is sketched out below. Meanwhile to obtain your auspicious and inauspicious directions please refer to Ch.9 which deals with the formula for calculating auspicious and inauspicious directions.

This end is fitted into the wall socket. It is NOT this end which we are talking about.

This end is joined to the appliance, and it is this end which should be entering the appliance from the auspicious direction

Let the direction of the arrow be your auspicious direction.

If the gas cooker is the main cooking appliance then make sure the gas enters the cooker FROM one of your good directions.

In kitchen layouts, the fire and water elements should not be in conflict

 Cooking stoves are of the fire element

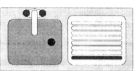 Kitchen sinks and Basins are of the water element

When arranging the layout of furniture and the placement of appliances in the kitchen, remember that fire and water are naturally opposing forces. Placing the kitchen sink right next to the stove or oven cannot be harmonious, and thus will not create good feng shui. This is because water destroys fire, the cooking medium ... in the same way and using the same analysis, it is also not advisable to place the refrigerator right next to the oven.

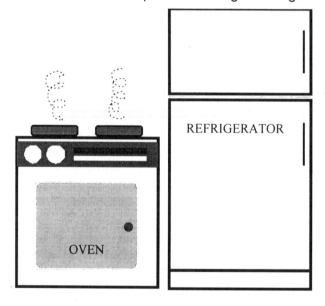

If the refrigerator is located next to the cooker, the clash of elements is considered to be quite severe. If your kitchen is very small, it is acceptable to place them opposite to each other but they should NEVER be next to each other.

... and beware fire at heaven's gate !!

It is important to remember that the stove should never be placed in the <u>NORTHWEST</u> of the kitchen, and of the home itself. This is the place of the home which represents heaven as symbolized by the trigram **chien**. If the stove is placed at *heaven's gate* ie in the Northwest, not only will success be elusive for the head of the household, but the house itself could catch fire and burn down.

Exposed shelves in the kitchen
create *bad chi*, and must be closed up

Here are three examples of kitchen arrangements with varying quality of feng shui... Notice that in all three kitchens the cabinets and shelves are closed with doors. This creates good vibrations in the kitchen. But then note the placement of sinks vis a vis the cookers, and the effect of windows and protruding tables.

Hanging dried onions and garlics above your head is discouraged.

Hanging pots and pans over the work area is also not advisable. This symbolises inbalance and problems with the mind.

This kitchen is bright and airy. It has excellent feng shui with good wide windows and ample space for movement.

159

Toilets and Bathrooms

For years, I wanted a spacious and large bathroom. For me it seemed to symbolize the epitome of luxury ... and then I discovered the feng shui significance of toilets and bathrooms. I was told over and over by feng shui experts to always keep all my toilet doors closed, and to keep my toilets and bathrooms small and insignificant.

And then I further discovered that in old Chinese homes, the kind of homes one finds in the exclusive suburbs of the great cities of China - Beijing, Shanghai and Canton - I found that these old family homes did not have toilets ... and I also discovered that on the farms where the poorer people lived, toilets were always located a little way away from the home. Why ?

 It seems that toilets are bad news from a feng shui perspective, and that the pernicious energy created in toilets can cause havoc to one's luck, and depending where the toilets are located the kind of luck affected varies.

Modern toilet luxuries, like the above can cause extreme feng shui problems if they happen to be located in the wrong places within the home.

If toilet is located in:	... the effect is:
NORTH	Bad luck in your career. Promotions hard to come by, and there are few opportunities !
SOUTH	Bad reputation. Respect is hard to come by.
EAST	Health suffers. Problems could be severe.
WEST	Bad luck for the children of the household.
CENTER	There is discord and bad luck in the family
NORTHEAST	Educational pursuits have little luck.
SOUTHEAST	There could be extreme bad luck in money matters. Income suffers.
NORTHWEST	Mentor luck will be totally lacking. Do not expect help from your superiors.
SOUTHWEST	Marriage luck suffers and singles have a hard time finding love and romance.

Feng shui cures for toilets
in the wrong places

From the foregoing table, it would seem that toilets are such bad news there is simply no place for them anywhere in the house. So what is there to do, especially since they are a necessity of life itself. The solution really is to keep toilets and bathrooms as small as possible so that they do not occupy the entire grid of any corner.

In addition it is also possible to use boulders which belong to the earth element to symbolically press down on the bad luck that is caused by toilets. This method is especially useful if the toilet is located **in the SOUTHWEST, CENTER and NORTHEAST**

Place a large **boulder** in the toilet or build a **low wall** which symbolically separates the toilet from the rest of the bathroom.

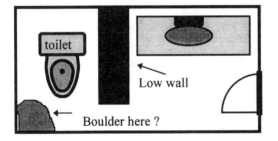

toilet

Low wall

Boulder here ?

These three corners of any home belong to the earth element, and boulders and walls, which can be said to belong to this element will have enough strength to press down on the *bad chi* of the toilet.

For toilets located in the WEST and NORTHWEST

Hang a really large **windchime** inside the toilet, or actually place a large metal **water tank** on top of the toilet itself. This presses down on the bad luck of the toilet.

For toilets located in other sectors, the only really effective way to reduce the *negative chi* is to keep the toilet doors closed. And if the toilet is located near the main door, it is necessary to make sure the door into the toilet is NOT · directly facing the main door. If it is vital to move the toilet door to another wall.

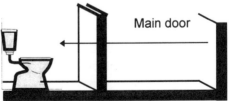

Main door

Toilet door in this example should be moved to another wall.

Store rooms & garages

These rooms are of lesser importance in terms of feng shui. Their significance lies in the fact that if they happen to be located in one of your important directions then store rooms and garages represent a waste of lucky floor space.

Store rooms are lifeless areas where residents seldom visit. Thus *yin* energy does tend to collect in such rooms, and it is always a good idea to check on such rooms regularly, Air them, tidy them and generally keep them clean so that energy does not have a chance to get stale or pernicious.

If store rooms are used to keep brooms and mops, make sure the door to the store room is kept closed at all times.

Garages fall into the same category as store rooms except that here the energy is more *yang* than *yin* since cars are used on a daily basis. But garages are regarded as empty rooms ie rooms which have no feng shui substance ... so that bedrooms or other important rooms that lie above garages are deemed to be seriously lacking in support. Bad feng shui is thus caused simply by locating the room directly above a garage. The best type of garages are those which are kept separate from the house itself.

Basement garages of multi level buildings which are underground are deemed to be better than garages that are placed on the *ground* or *in between* floors. In fact, buildings which have the entire ground level used as garages or as places to park cars, are creating excessively bad feng shui for the entire building since this symbolize that the building is seriously lacking foundation.

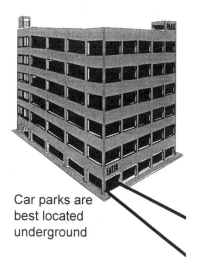

Car parks are best located underground

Staircases and Ceilings

When reviewing the feng shui of staircases there are several important rules to observe:

1. Staircases should **never start directly in front of the main door**. This configuration is disastrous and the longer and higher the staircase the more severe will be the bad luck. In fact staircases should never start nor end in front of a door.

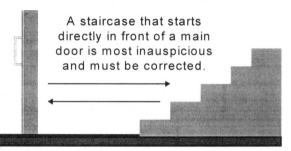

A staircase that starts directly in front of a main door is most inauspicious and must be corrected.

2. Staircases should **never be spiral**, to the extent that it resembles a cork screw. Curved staircases on the other hand are deemed to be auspicious.

3. Staircases **should have solid steps**. The steps should not have hollows or be cantilevered since this causes the flow of *chi* to seep through ... thereby depriving the upper floors of good fortune.

4. Staircases should never start or end in front of a toilet. If you have this problem, the first thing to do is keep the toilet door closed at all times. Then see if you can place a screen in front of the staircase. If you cannot, then try **to rebuild the last three steps of the staircase** so it no longer points at the toilet.

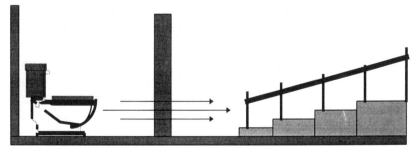

Three easy ways to correct
bad staircase feng shui

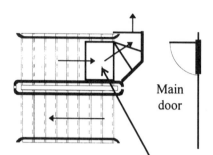

A very effective way of handling a staircase which faces the main front door is to re build the last few steps of the staircase in such a way that the staircase is actually diverted towards a different direction, as shown.

Create a small landing to make it easy for the staircase to be turned.

If there is sufficient space, another effective method to correct a wrongly placed staircase is to place a sold screen in between. This method also works if there is a toilet directly facing the main door. The screen should be solid. A thin curtain is not strong enough to block.

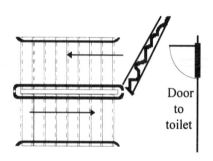

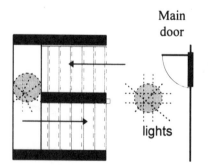

When all things fail, you can resort to installing bright lights at the start of the staircase (in the foyer) and also on the landing. A good cluster of lights serves to lift up the energy, in the process transforming any bad energy into healthy auspicious energy.

Some examples of staircases
that are best avoided

This staircase resembles teeth in the living room. Grills painted black against a white background are not a good idea. Staircases should be solid.

The landing below this staircase is empty. This is an example of lack of substance below the pathway upstairs. Close up and use as a store-room.

This staircase looks very good. It is flanked by 2 pillars and an arched doorway. It is also next to the main door without confronting it. Excellent.

The simple rule on ceilings
is to keep them simple !

There are some genuinely attractive ceiling designs which enhance a room tremendously, but in the interests of feng shui, ceilings are best kept simple. If you want to have patterns, keep them circular and basic rather than angular and too elaborate. Strenuously avoid **sloping ceilings** especially where the lower end of the slope is the where the door is located.

Also avoid **ridged ceilings,** and be on the lookout for exposed or protruding **overhead beams**. Make certain there are no doors, no beds and no chairs and sofas placed under such beams.

Structural beams are especially harmful especially in multi.level apartment blocks, since there are many similar beams one on top of the other ...

Examples of harmful ceiling designs, above left – a slanted ceiling, above right – glassed opening above foyer and below, exposed overhead beams create severe *shar chi.*

It is useful to always be alert to what is directly upstairs

Much of the fine tuning in feng shui involves living in a state of awareness and sensitivity to your surroundings. One area of awareness which helps to improve the feng shui of a multi level home, or apartment is to try and know what lies directly above your bed, your sofa, your dining table, your favorite chair and your stove. If these pieces of furniture are being hit by heavy furniture or toilets from above, the energy created is harmful. How severe it is depends on how heavy the pressure of the bad energy is, and also how directly you are getting hit. It is thus advisable to investigate these matters if you are regularly suffering from anger, temper tantrums, headaches and illnesses.

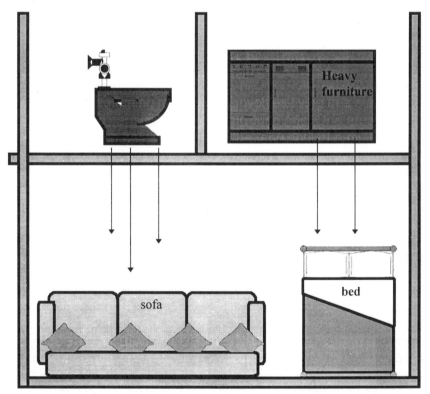

Remember that the pernicious energy of heavy objects and harmful features from the floor above can sometimes penetrate through the floors and cause hurt ... better to move the bed or sofa away.

8 ENHANCING THE LIVING SPACE

metal

fire earth

wood

applying five element theory

water

Feng shui is about protecting the home from bad vibes. It is also about consciously creating good energy, and the best way to do this is to apply the theory of the five elements in a practical way. Readers should by now be thoroughly familiar with two basic aspects of feng shui and these are that:

1. Every corner of the home is represented by one of the elements.
2. Every corner of the home also represents one of life's aspirations.

Please refer to pages 24 and 39 to revise on the tables which show this co - relation. When we apply element theory with a view to actively improving our luck, then strengthening the feng shui of each and every corner will embellish different aspects of our luck. At the same time it is necessary to be mindful of the **Productive** and **Destructive** cycles of the five elements because this tells us what is NOT suitable in each of the corners !

Elements must always be in harmony. Discordant notes caused by clashing elements create disharmony and does no good for the feng shui. Next, it is also necessary to note that not all the matching symbols of the elements are suitable for every room. For example, while plants and flowers are of the wood element, placing them in the bedroom is not auspicious. Similarly while water may be an excellent energizer for the North, placing water features in the bedroom cause more harm than good.
Usually the best place to practice your feng shui enhancing techniques is the living room where representations of all five elements can be placed in their respective matching corners thereby creating extremely favorable flows of energy within the home. When applying these enhancing techniques, it is perfectly fine to use your personal creativity. Use shapes and colors as well as objects, paintings, statues, works of art and other decorative items to magnify the harmonious flows of energy.

To identify each of the corners of the home in terms of the compass, stand in the center of the home and take your directions. Then mark out the eight corners by superimposing the nine sector grid onto a floor plan of the entire home. Do the same for each and every room whose feng shui you wish to intensify or restore. There will thus be two aspects of this same exercise. First take the *whole home* view, and then take each room separately. Then enhance the corners according to the compass orientation of each of the eight corners. This is illustrated below.

Southeast enhance this corner with the wood element	**SOUTH** enhance this corner with fire element ie lights, candles etc. Use red	**Southwest** enhance this corner with the earth element
EAST enhance this corner with wood. Use plants, flowers and green.	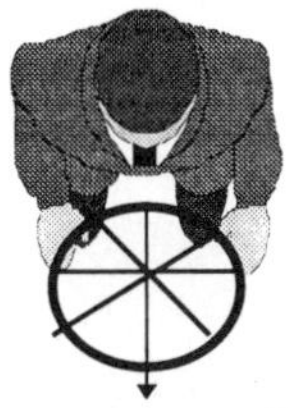 Take compass reading from the center of the home.	**WEST** enhance this corner with metal element ie bells, chimes. Use white.
Northeast enhance this corner with the earth element	**NORTH** enhance this corner with the water element	**Northwest** enhance this corner with the metal element

Identifying the heart of the home

Feng shui places emphasis on the *heart of the home*. This is basically the center of the home, and the feng shui of this part of the home affects the rest of the home. Thus attention should be paid to this part of the home.

Generally the best rooms to be located in the center of your home should be rooms which represent the socializing place for the whole family - this means the dining room or the family room. If the heart of the home is where all members of the family, OR where all residents of the building congregate, then the feng shui is healthy and very *yang* !

If the *heart of the home* is always silent (e.g. when the store room is located here) OR is repeatedly hit by *shar chi* (ie when a toilet is located here) OR has a sense of emptiness (e.g. when an empty air well is located here) the feng shui of the entire home gets affected.

The way to activate and enhance the center of your home is to create some sort of social corner here, complete with music, laughter and interactive happiness. Let the heart of your home be a place of healthy *yang* energy.

If the dining room is located in the center of the home, the feng shui is auspicious. Decorate the room in **earth** colors !

protecting and enhancing

It is important to understand the difference between **protecting** and **enhancing** in feng shui. Both concepts are equally important and neither should be ignored if you really want to have good feng shui. This is because it is as important to be protected against bad feng shui as it is to consciously create good feng shui.

It is important to understand that no matter how well you have calculated your compass formulas, and how accurately you have measured your feng shui dimensions, if your home, or any place that you sit, sleep or eat is being affected by bad vibes caused by secret poison arrows, then all your carefully crafted feng shui could well fly out the window ! In this context, **protection** becomes significant. As do cures and corrections.

But stopping short at protecting against bad feng shui will not bring you the kind of huge good fortune you are looking for, and particularly, for the specific types of luck you want. This can only be achieved when you start to activate, to energize and to **enhance** explicit areas of luck you feel you need or require.

But when it comes to a choice between protecting and enhancing, it is more important to protect than to enhance ! You need to understand that it is seldom possible to get everything right or according to feng shui principles and guidelines. There is always a need for some sort of compromise. For example, perhaps in tapping your most auspicious directions you might be directly facing a *poison arrow* ... in which case it is better to forgo tapping your best direction since facing the poison arrow destroys the good luck of the auspicious direction anyway !

If you can implement even 60 to 70 % of *all* the feng shui features you identify around your living space, that is already very good. It is also not necessary to fret about certain configurations which you feel may not be ideal.

Again, I stress the fact that almost everyone has to put up with some *less than ideal* feng shui features which they cannot do anything about. So don't fret.

When I speak of energizing the cosmic breath, I am referring to the **energies** that surround your living space. When you start to practice feng shui, you will instinctively develop increasing awareness of your space, your surroundings, and the greater environments around your place of work, your place of leisure and your place of rest. These energies, which modern science has already confirmed does exist, is generally referred to in feng shui terms as the **dragon's cosmic breath** OR **chi**, the inner breath, the potent breath, the subtle breath - which is invisible, intangible and yet exceedingly potent and powerful.

Feng shui is all about capturing, accumulating and storing the good cosmic breath, what is termed **sheng chi** in the language of feng shui. This good cosmic breath brings exceedingly good fortune. It brings success, recognition, prosperity and harmony.

Feng shui is also about avoiding, deflecting and dissolving the *killing breath*, what is termed **shar chi** because this type of energies are equally powerful and potent but they bring disaster, loss and all sorts of misfortunes.
In developing awareness of surroundings it is useful therefore to know about the characteristics of *sheng chi* and *shar chi* since this knowledge will make better, your practice of feng shui.

SHENG CHI
always moves slowly, in a meandering fashion,
and it accumulates in places where there is yin yang balance, and where there is element harmony.

SHAR CHI
always travels in straight lines, and are created by angular or sharp edges. Shar chi also exists where there is yin yang imbalance, and where the destructive cycle of the elements are activated.

 Plants and flowers belong to the wood element, and they exhibit the main characteristic of WOOD which is the only *growth* element in the basket of five elements.

Here are some general guidelines to bear in mind when you place plants in corners of your home for feng shui purposes.

1. Ideally the plants and flowers should be live plants. If you cannot find live plants, you can use fake plants, and there are many wonderful silk flowers and fake trees which look very lifelike. These can be used for feng shui purposes. BUT do not display dead, or dried plants since these emanate a great deal of *yin* energy, and are usually unsuitable for *yang* dwellings.

2. If you keep live plants, please always make sure that they are healthy and vibrant looking. If your plants turn yellow and sickly, it is better to throw them out and replace with a new plant. Sick plants also give off *yin* energy.

3. Plants are best placed in the living room and dining room and never in the kitchens or bedrooms. When plants are placed in the bedroom, there will be excessive yang energy in a room of rest. Flowers in the bedroom are also not encouraged in feng shui unless there is a sick person there who would benefit from the yang energy of the flowers. These are feng shui subtleties which fine tune the practice.

4. Plants can be placed in any corner of the room except the *earth* element corners ie the Southwest, the Center and the Northeast. This is due to the fact that wood destroys earth. In the garden however, the plants in the earth corners are balanced out by the placement of rocks used in landscaping. Rocks (earth) strengthen the earth element.

5. Finally, never overdo things. Do not create imbalance by having too many plants inside the home. The wood element could create havoc when in too much abundance.

The best way of energizing and strengthening the FIRE element is to use bright lights (or candles). The fire element is also said to raise the *sheng chi* upwards, and as such, lights can also be used to correct a broad range of feng shui ailments.

Here are some general guidelines in the use of lights in feng shui.

1. Lights are best placed in the South corner of any room, or of the home itself since this is the corner of the fire element. In addition however, lights also strengthen the earth corners since fire produces earth. the earth corners are Southwest, Northeast and the center of the home.

2. Irrespective of orientations, lights are also ideal for expanding and *raising the chi* in cramped corners and in small foyers that need to be enlarged.

3. Lights can also be used to generate vital *yang* energies into lifeless rooms ie rooms that are seldom used, or which recently had a very ill person residing. Indeed whenever there is a lack of *yang* energy, just installing a light should correct the problem.

4. Lights should never be glaring. But they should be bright. Crystal chandeliers are said to be good feng shui because they are bright but not glaring. Also such lights combine the fire with the earth element, thereby creating harmony.

5. It is excellent feng shui to have a bright light just directly in front of the main door, both on the inside and on the outside. This encourages and attracts the *good luck chi* into the home.

6. Lights can be used to correct inauspicious feng shui caused by missing corners in U shaped and L shaped houses. In such instances a tall light should be placed at the missing corner to *regularize* the shape of the home.

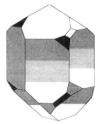

The EARTH element has direct relevance in the practice of feng shui because this science is all about tapping into the prosperity secrets of the earth. The Southwest is the place of <u>big earth</u> as symbolized by the trigram KUN which represents *mother earth.* The Northeast represents small earth.

Here are some important general guidelines on the use of earth element objects like crystals and rocks.

1. Natural quartz and other crystals are probably one of the best feng shui energizing objects easily available to everyone. If you can afford them, get these crystals in rock form - they can be the purple amethysts, the yellow citrines or the watermelon colored tourmalines and so forth ... Place them in earth corners which are the Southwest, Northeast and the center.

2. If your main door, or the entrance to your shop or office faces any one of the earth directions, OR is located in any one of the earth sectors, then place a beautiful, and deep crystal directly in front of the door ... if your crystal has a deep pocket ie it looks like a kind of container, this is even better since it then symbolically attracts and stores all the good luck entering the home.

3. Hang a small faceted lead crystal (the type that is man made, and which are used in chandeliers) near windows to catch the rays of the morning sun. The cut crystal will break the rays of sunlight into wonderful *yang energy rainbows* that bring loads of good luck into the home. This kind of luck enhancing technique is especially potent in the living room.

4. Place a solid crystal ball (it does not matter about the size) on a table in the Southwest of your living room to enhance relationship and romance luck, and in the Northeast of a bedroom to embellish the occupant's educational luck.

water features to enhance the water element

Water features are generally associated with increased prosperity, added income and financial success. To the Chinese water has always been associated with wealth so that activating water in the correct corners of the home does offer the promise of enhanced money luck.

Here are the guidelines on the use of water features like fish bowls, aquariums and even miniature fountains within the home.

1. Place a small aquarium in the Southeast to activate money luck. This is the sector that governs financial success, and because its element is wood, placing a water feature here with fish (itself a good fortune symbol) is excellent for creating income luck (water produce wood). As to what type of fish, consider the goldfish, any variety of carp and even the humble little guppy.

2. Place a water bowl in the North of the home, or of the living room, and keep a small *terrapin* (or water tortoise). Keep a single terrapin or tortoise since the numeral associated with the North is ! This is a potent feng shui enhancing tip.

3. Hang a painting which has a body of water in it, near the vicinity of your main door - landscape paintings with lakes, waterfalls and rivers are ideal. Placing something like this in the foyer of the home suggests good fortune BUT do place such paintings on the left hand side of the door. If you have a real water feature near the main door, again follow this guideline. Let the water feature be on the left hand side of the main door. Otherwise the man of the household will have a roving eye, and could even end up having multiple wives.

4. Water features in the home should have clean water at all times. Do not let the water get stale, stagnant or polluted. It is best when there is a constant movement in the water.

windchimes to enhance the metal element

 The metal element corners of the home are the **West** and the **Northwest** corners, and these are places within the home that benefit most from the hanging of metal windchimes - *copper, aluminum and steel*, which are especially potent when there are also feng shui defects to be corrected.

Here are the general guidelines in the use of windchimes

1. Make sure the windchimes you use for feng shui reasons, have **hollow** rods. When the rods are solid they do not have the ability to channel *chi* upwards, and are thus unsuitable for feng shui.

2. As to the number of rods, the best number of rods to have is 6, 7, 8 or 9. These are the lucky numbers during this feng shui period which lasts until the year 2003. There are certain schools which contend that having 5 rods is unlucky.

3. Use only metal windchimes in the West and Northwest corners. Use ceramic windchimes for the earth corners and wood windchimes for the wood corners.

4. Do not confuse the use of mobiles with windchimes. Hanging mobiles is a decorative feature, but it has no feng shui effect whatsoever. Mobiles of fish and bells however, may be deemed to symbolize good fortune.

5. Use windchimes to correct feng shui defects like hanging them in front of a **protruding corner**; or hung off an exposed **overhead beam**, or to combat a threatening **poison arrow** which is hitting the main door. The windchime used under such circumstances is enormously effective in dissolving bad *shar chi* created. By hanging just such a windchime in front of my main door, a particularly annoying coconut tree on the road directly opposite my main door, shriveled and died of its own accord ! The windchime I used, had rods 18 inches long.

combining the elements

If you understand the true nature of the 5 element theory, you will also understand that it is not any single element per se that is important or unimportant - but rather the entire <u>basket of elements</u> that represent the most auspicious of circumstance. Thus when you activate every corner of the home, you will in effect have introduced a good balance of all five elements into the home. This represents good feng shui.

When there is an insufficiency of one or several of the elements, OR when one particular element is missing, it has to be corrected since the lack of even one element will seriously cause imbalance. Thus even while feng shui advocates the energizing of the various corners of a home according to the designated element of each of the corners, in the final analysis, a good balance and proportion of all five elements within the home is vital.

The main point to ensure is that the Destructive Cycle of elements is always observed and taken note of so that they do not create discordant notes within the home.

an example on how to activate a whole basket of elements

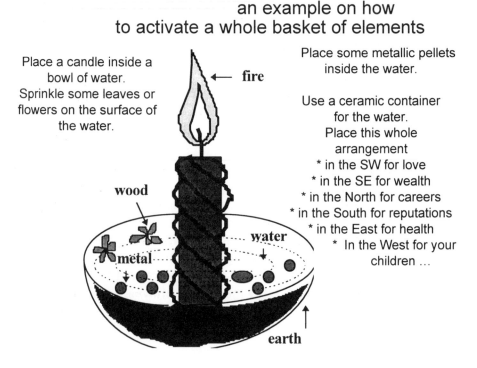

Place a candle inside a bowl of water. Sprinkle some leaves or flowers on the surface of the water.

fire

Place some metallic pellets inside the water.

Use a ceramic container for the water.
Place this whole arrangement
* in the SW for love
* in the SE for wealth
* in the North for careers
* in the South for reputations
* in the East for health
* In the West for your children …

wood

metal

water

earth

fine tuning the basics yourself

There are **three main steps** to achieving good feng shui:

1. Diagnosing what, if anything is wrong
2. Correcting any feng shui defects diagnosed
3. Actively creating good feng shui.

In applying these three steps of **diagnosis, correction** and **enhancement** of feng shui, there will arise a multiple array of uncertainty and confusion. When in doubt, always go back to the basics and fine tune what is required by systematically applying the fundamentals of the science.

Thus, always relate the problem diagnosed to the key aspects of landscape and environmental feng shui. Check against the main rules of feng shui, and make sure nothing harmful is hurting the home. Also check the orientations of the home and compare the major directions to what is best for each of the individuals who live in the home according to the compass formulas.

Fine tuning of the basics also call for a systematic mental investigation of all the visible yin and yang energies present within the home, and a keen awareness of the harmony or disharmony of elements within the home. It is impossible to get everything correct at the start, simply because feng shui is affected by every feature and object within the home.

Feng shui is also not static - it is dynamic and it changes because the energy in the living space changes according to the seasons, to the weather and with the way the winds blow, the rains fall and the sun shines ! Feng shui is best applied step by step - which is why I advocate that you do it yourself. No expert, no matter how good, can spot and get everything right in one visit. Nor can he or she know how the house is affected by the morning sun and the evening breeze ... study the basics and then apply the concepts and the formulas yourself. Finally do remember that professional feng shui men *can* get things wrong. Even the most competent of professionals have their off days. But when **you** do your own feng shui, you will have a vested interest in getting things right !

In the proliferation of feng shui offerings that is now becoming increasingly available, my sympathies are with the amateur practitioner who has no way of knowing what is and what is not feng shui. Even before addressing the legitimate issue of choosing between different methods and between applying different formulas, it is important to first of all state quite categorically what is and what is not feng shui.

So called cleansing of the the living space is NOT feng shui !

I do recognize that there may be homes which suffer from a surfeit of negative or harmful energies; that there are haunted houses; that there are homes wherein *naughty* spirits may well reside. Such homes DO need clearing ! What is needed in such circumstances could well be a spiritual cleansing requiring the help of your priest. But the rituals of spiritual cleansing IS NOT feng shui ! It is vital that one does not confuse the science of feng shui with spiritual cleansing !

Feng shui prescribes methods and guidelines of orientating your home, and the placement of things within your home to create good energy. It involves the harmonious blending of the subtle energies within the environment. It is **not** of, or by itself a spiritual practice, and therefore should not be seen as such.

So when we speak of choosing between different methods or different schools of feng shui, I am referring to the dilemma we can often have to face when feng shui advice is contrary. This arises when the application of Compass school methods clash with the application of Form school methods. In other words, when, in trying to tap one's auspicious direction, one gets confronted with a form school feng shui taboo. In such a circumstance, which method does one follow ?

The general guideline is to put priority on being defensive ! Thus if in applying any recommendation, one gets inadvertently hit by some dangerous configuration, then it is best to adopt a defensive posture. Go for the action or arrangement which protects.

180

9 USING FORMULA FENG SHUI

the pa kua lo shu formula

This is a powerful compass school formula taken from the classical texts for determining the most auspicious directions and locations according to **birth dates** and **gender.** The formula offers a personalized method of determining auspicious and inauspicious directions, and its great value lies in its tremendous potency and its incredible ease of practice.

The formula is easy to apply but there are many different ways of using it. Indeed, I have written an entire book on just this formula alone because there are so many different permutations and so much feng shui relevance to the formula.

Many of the applications of the formula have been dealt with throughout this book, where ever it has been of relevance. This chapter focuses directly onto the formula itself; ie the method of computation for determining every individual's auspicious and inauspicious direction and location within the home.

The pa kua lo shu formula

To determine your personal auspicious and inauspicious directions, you must **first work out your personal KUA numbers.** The calculation of your personal KUA number requires your year of birth and your gender. But the year of birth used must first be converted into the equivalent year according to the lunar calendar

 The formula for men:

Take the year of birth
Add the last two digits
Reduce to a single number
Deduct from 10.
<u>Example:</u> Year of birth 1936
3+6=9 and 10-9=1
so the KUA number is 1.

 The formula for women

Take the year of birth
Add the last two digits
Reduce to a single number
Add 5.
Example: Year of birth 1945
4+5=9; 9+5=14; 1+4=5
so the KUA number is 5

Once you have discovered your KUA number from the formula on the preceding page you will be able to discover whether you are an EAST group or a WEST group person. According to this method of feng shui, everyone is either an East group or a West group person, and generally East group people are extremely compatible with other East group people and extremely incompatible with West group people ! The same is true for West group people. To find out if you are an East or West group person, simply match your KUA numbers according to the groups below.

EAST

GROUP people have KUA numbers 1, 3, 4, and 9

WEST

GROUP people have KUA numbers 5, 2, 6, 7 and 8

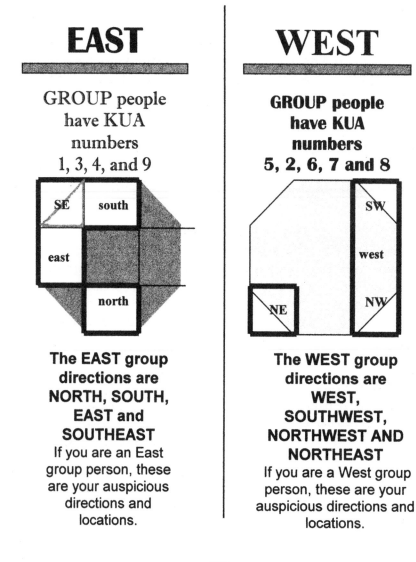

The EAST group directions are NORTH, SOUTH, EAST and SOUTHEAST
If you are an East group person, these are your auspicious directions and locations.

The WEST group directions are WEST, SOUTHWEST, NORTHWEST AND NORTHEAST
If you are a West group person, these are your auspicious directions and locations.

Four lucky and four unlucky directions

According to this formula, there are four lucky and four unlucky directions for each person, and it is easy to remember because:

■ if you are an East group person your lucky directions are the East group directions and your unlucky directions are the West group directions.

■ if you are a West group person your lucky directions are the West group directions and your unlucky directions are the East group directions.

The lucky and unlucky directions are further broken down into specific levels of good and bad luck. Thus each of the eight main directions of the compass represent either a specific type of good luck, or a specific level of bad luck. Each of the KUA numbers thus allow these specific types of good and bad luck to be spelt out. needless to say, in knowing the intensity of good or bad luck associated with each direction, this compass formula allows the feng shui that is applied to one's living space to be extremely finely tuned.

This is because the directions have many different applications, with the most obvious being the orientation of the main and secondary doors, the sleeping directions and locations, the eating direction, the working directions and locations, the travel directions and much more besides.

SOME APPLICATION OF LUCKY DIRECTIONS.

EATING   SLEEPING   STUDYING   WORKING

Those of you who want to go deeper into this formula can get my book devoted exclusively to this formula entitled APPLIED PA KUA LO SHU FENG SHUI. In basic feng shui however, it is more than sufficient simply to be in possession of one's detailed lucky and unlucky directions.

> If your KUA number is **1, 3, 4 or 9,** you are an East group person and your detailed lucky and unlucky directions are as set down in the table below as follows.
> These are applicable for both male and female.

KUA → NUMBERS	1	3	4	9
BEST DIRECTION	southeast	south	north	east
HEALTH DIRECTION	east	north	south	southeast
ROMANCE DIRECTION	south	southeast	east	north
PERSONAL GROWTH DIRECTION	north	east	southeast	south
UNLUCKY DIRECTION	west	southwest	northwest	northeast
FIVE GHOSTS DIRECTION	northeast	northwest	southwest	west
SIX KILLINGS DIRECTION	northwest	northeast	west	southwest
TOTAL LOSS DIRECTION	southwest	west	northeast	northwest

Use the above table to determine which specific direction you should activate for specific types of good luck, and also to determine how bad, each of the west group direction is for you. Please note for instance that if your main door faces your **total loss** direction, it is likely that bad luck will definitely befall you. Once you know what your unlucky directions are, you will be able to tell immediately whether a particular house will be lucky or unlucky for you simply by checking the orientation of the main front door.

If your KUA number is either 5, 2, 6, 7, or 8 you are a west group person and your detailed lucky and unlucky directions are set down below as follows.

KUA NUMBERS	5 MALE	5 FEMALE	2 for ALL	6 for ALL	7 for ALL	8 for ALL
BEST DIRECTION	NE	SW	NE	W	NW	SW
HEALTH DIRECTION	W	NW	W	NE	SW	NW
ROMANCE DIRECTION	NW	W	NW	SW	NE	W
PERSONAL GROWTH DIRECTION	SW	NE	SW	NW	W	NE
UNLUCKY DIRECTION	E	S	E	SE	N	S
FIVE GHOSTS DIRECTION	SE	N	SE	E	S	N
SIX KILLINGS DIRECTION	S	E	S	N	SE	E
TOTAL LOSS DIRECTION	N	SE	N	S	E	SE

Use the above table to determine your **best sleeping direction**. Depending on what kind of luck you wish to activate, let your head be pointed towards the direction that is most appropriate to your particular aspiration. Thus if you wish to activate family or romance luck, or if you want to start a family and seem to be having a hard time, or if your marriage is not going quite right, then sleep with your head pointed towards your romance direction as shown in the sketch on the right.

This is the way to take direction when sleeping

As must be obvious by now, you can use the *pa kua lo shu* formula of directions and orientations to activate particular aspirations. It does not matter if you are west or east group. The way to activate your direction is simply to make sure you are using the direction that is specifically suited to exactly the kind of luck you want, based on your date of birth and your KUA number !

If you wish to have success at work,
or if you want that promotion, or if you want to make your company more profitable, then sit at your work desk directly facing your best direction.

If you are having health problems, or you constantly succumb to viruses, or you simply cannot rest well at nights, then you should try to sleep with your head pointed to your heath direction and you should eat facing your health direction.

If you wish to study better, and improve your exam grades then you should sit at your desk facing your personal growth direction, and try to take your exams facing this direction. if you cannot tap into this direction, then try to at least sit facing at least one of your four lucky directions.

If for some reason you are unable to sleep, sit or work facing the direction you want (and this is more than likely), then you should try to tap, at least one of your four auspicious directions.
This is simply to ensure that you do not sit or sleep, work or study facing any one of your inauspicious directions, two of which can be deadly indeed. The *six killings* direction and the *total loss* direction are to be feared since these are considered both harmful and malevolent.

GETTING YOUR KUA NUMBER

The Chinese calendar is made up of 60 year cycles which are differentiated according to *heavenly stems* and *earthly branches* ! To obtain your KUA number, you need to first determine your YEAR of birth according to the lunar calendar. You get this by noting the cut off dates for each new year. Thus if you were born on Feb 5th 1975 your year of birth is **not** 1975 but is instead 1974. Again, if you were born on Jan 21st 1987, then your lunar year of birth is not 1987 but is 1986. Armed with your year of birth you can proceed to calculate your KUA number from the formula on Page 181

ANIMAL	**WESTERN CALENDAR DATES**	**YEAR ELEMENT**
RAT (water)	Feb 18, 1912 - Feb 5, 1913	water
OX (earth)	Feb 6, 1913 - Jan 25, 1914	water
TIGER (wood)	Jan 26, 1914 - Feb 13, 1915	wood
RABBIT(wood)	Feb 14, 1915 - Feb 2, 1916	wood
DRAGON (earth)	Feb 3, 1916 - Jan 22, 1917	fire
SNAKE (fire)	Jan 23, 1917 - Feb 10, 1918	fire
HORSE (fire)	Feb 11, 1918 - Jan 31, 1919	earth
SHEEP (earth)	Feb 1, 1919 - Feb 19, 1920	earth
MONKEY(metal)	Feb 20, 1920 - Feb 7, 1921	metal
ROOSTER(metal)	Feb 8, 1921 - Jan 27, 1922	metal
DOG (earth)	Feb 28, 1922 - Feb 15, 1923	water
BOAR (water)	Feb 16th 1923 - Feb 4, 1924	water
✪ start of 60 year	cycle	
RAT (water)	Feb 5th 1924 - Jan 23, 1925	wood
OX (earth)	Jan 24, 1925 - Feb 12, 1926	wood
TIGER (wood)	Feb 13, 1926 - Feb 1, 1927	fire
RABBIT (wood)	Feb 2, 1927 - Jan 22, 1928	fire
DRAGON (earth)	Jan 23, 1928 - Feb 9, 1929	earth
SNAKE (fire)	Feb 10, 1929 - Jan 29, 1930	earth
HORSE (fire)	Jan 30 1930 - Feb 16, 1931	metal
SHEEP (earth)	Feb 17 1931 - Feb 5 1932	metal
MONKEY (metal)	Feb 6, 1932 - Jan 25, 1933	water
ROOSTER (metal)	Jan 26, 1933 - Feb 13, 1934	water
DOG (earth)	Feb 14, 1934 - Feb 3, 1935	wood
BOAR	Feb 4, 1935 - Jan 23, 1936	wood

ANIMAL	WESTERN CALENDAR DATES	YEAR ELEMENT
RAT (water)	Jan 24, 1936 - Feb 10, 1937	Fire
OX (earth)	Feb 11, 1937 - Jan 30, 1938	Fire
TIGER (wood)	Jan 31, 1938 - Feb 18, 1939	Earth
RABBIT(wood)	Feb 19, 1939 - Feb 7, 1940	Earth
DRAGON(earth)	Feb 8, 1940 - Jan 26, 1941	Metal
SNAKE (fire)	Jan 27, 1941 - Feb 14, 1942	Metal
HORSE (fire)	Feb 15, 1942 - Feb 4, 1943	Water
SHEEP (earth)	Feb 5, 1943 - Jan 24, 1944	Water
MONKEY (metal)	Jan 25 1944 - Feb 12 1945	Wood
ROOSTER (metal)	Feb 13, 1945 - Feb 1, 1946	Wood
DOG (earth)	Feb 2, 1946 - Jan 21, 1947	Fire
BOAR (water)	Jan 22, 1947 - Feb 9, 1948	Fire
RAT (water)	Feb 10, 1948 - Jan 28, 1949	Earth
OX(earth)	Jan 29 1949 - Feb 16, 1950	Earth
TIGER (wood)	Feb 17, 1950 - Feb 5, 1951	Metal
RABBIT (wood)	Feb 6, 1951 - Jan 26, 1952	Metal
DRAGON (earth)	Jan 27, 1952 - Feb 13, 1953	Water
SNAKE (fire)	Feb 14, 1953 - Feb 2, 1954	Water
HORSE (fire)	Feb 3, 1954 - Jan 23, 1955	Wood
SHEEP (earth)	Jan 24, 1955 - Feb 11 1956	Wood
MONKEY (metal)	Feb 12, 1956 - Jan 30 1957	Fire
ROOSTER (metal)	Jan 31, 1957 - Feb 17, 1958	Fire
DOG (earth)	Feb 18, 1958 - Feb 7, 1959	Earth
BOAR (water)	Feb 8, 1959 - Jan 27, 1960	Earth
RAT (water)	Jan 28, 1960 - Feb 14, 1961	Metal
OX (earth)	Feb 15, 1961 - Feb 4, 1962	Metal
TIGER (wood)	Feb 5, 1962 - Jan 24, 1963	Water
RABBIT (wood)	Jan 25, 1963 - Feb 12, 1964	Water
DRAGON (earth)	Feb 13, 1964 - Feb 1, 1965	Wood
SNAKE (fire)	Feb 2, 1965 - Jan 20, 1966	Wood
HORSE (fire)	Jan 21 1966 - Feb 8, 1967	Fire
SHEEP (earth)	Feb 9 1967 - Jan 29, 1968	Fire
MONKEY (metal)	Jan 30, 1968 - Feb 16, 1969	Earth
ROOSTER (metal)	Feb 17, 1969 - Feb 5, 1970	Earth
DOG (earth)	Feb 6 1970 - Jan 26, 1971	Metal
BOAR (water)	Jan 27, 1971 - Feb 14 1972	Metal

ANIMAL	WESTERN CALENDAR DATES	YEAR ELEMENT
RAT (water)	Feb 15, 1972 - Feb 2, 1973	Water
OX (earth)	Feb 3, 1973 - Jan 22, 1974	Water
TIGER (wood)	Jan 23, 1974 - Feb 10, 1975	Wood
RABBIT (wood)	Feb 11, 1975 - Jan 30, 1976	Wood
DRAGON (earth)	Jan 31, 1976 - Feb 17, 1977	Fire
SNAKE (fire)	Feb 18, 1977 - Feb 6, 1978	Fire
HORSE (fire)	Feb 7, 1978 - Jan 27, 1979	Earth
SHEEP (earth)	Jan 28, 1979 - Feb 15, 1980	Earth
MONKEY (metal)	Feb 16, 1980 - Feb 4, 1981	Metal
ROOSTER (metal)	Feb 5. 1981 - Jan 24, 1982	Metal
DOG (earth)	Jan 25, 1982 - Feb 12, 1983	Water
BOAR (water)	Feb 13, 1983 - Feb 1, 1984	Water
RAT (water)	Feb 2, 1984 - Feb 19, 1985	Wood
OX (earth)	Feb 20, 1985 - Feb 8, 1986	Wood
TIGER (wood)	Feb 9, 1986 - Jan 28, 1987	Fire
RABBIT (wood)	Jan 29, 1987 - Feb 16, 1988	Fire
DRAGON (earth)	Feb 17, 1988 - Feb 5, 1989	Earth
SNAKE (fire)	Feb 6, 1989 - Jan 26, 1990	Earth
HORSE (fire)	Jan 27, 1990 - Feb 14, 1991	Metal
SHEEP (earth)	Feb 15, 1991 - Feb 3, 1992	Metal
MONKEY (metal)	Feb 4, 1992 - Jan 22, 1993	Water
ROOSTER metal)	Jan 23, 1993 - Feb 9, 1994	Water
DOG (earth)	Feb 10, 1994 - Jan 30, 1995	Wood
BOAR (water)	Jan 31, 1995 - Feb 18, 1996	Wood
RAT (water)	Feb 19, 1996 - Feb 6, 1997	Fire
OX (earth)	Feb 7, 1997 - Jan 27, 1998	Fire
TIGER (wood)	Jan 28, 1998 - Feb 15, 1999	Earth
RABBIT (wood)	Feb 16, 1999 - Feb 4, 2000	Earth
DRAGON (earth)	Feb 5, 2000 - Jan 23, 2001,	Metal
SNAKE (fire)	Jan 24, 2001 - Feb 11, 2002	Metal
HORSE (fire)	Feb 12, 2002 - Jan 31, 2003	Water
SHEEP (earth)	Feb 1, 2003 - Jan 21, 2004	Water
MONKEY (metal)	Jan 22, 2004 - Feb 8, 2005	Wood
ROOSTER (metal)	Feb 9, 2005 - Jan 28, 2006	Wood
DOG (earth)	Jan 29, 2006 - Feb 17, 2007	Fire
BOAR (water)	Feb 18, 2007 - Feb 6, 2008	Fire

"To find happiness and avoid suffering, we should understand the principal cause and conditions that bring happiness, so we can practice them, and perceive those that bring suffering, so we can avoid them.

Correct feng-shui is an external condition that contributes to achieving harmony and success. Incorrect feng-shui brings disharmony. Therefore, it is important when one is building a new house to build according to feng-shui so that harmony prevails for many years. However, even though feng-shui can help in many ways, it is not the main cause of success and happiness in life. The main cause of all success and happiness is your own mind, is good karma, a positive, pure, healthy intention, a peaceful attitude toward life, the nature of which is non-attachment, non-ignorance, non-hatred and non-self centered mind.

What is karma ?
Karma is the mental factor. Karma is the principal cause of happiness and suffering. It is the inner cause. Karma is the mind.
The experience of enjoyment comes from the mind, which in turn comes from karma. Your present good rebirth with many opportunities to achieve happiness comes from good karma, your positive virtuous intention. Your mind is formless, colorless and shapeless and in taking its place in a fertilized human egg, creates the continuity of the physical body. The mind itself comes from its own previous continuity, the life before this one, the past life. And there are many past lives.

Good feng-shui depends on good karma. Success and happiness in this life and beyond this life up to the perfect fully completed bliss and peace of full enlightenment all depend on creating good karma, collecting merit, practising Dharma, and keeping your life attitude in pure, positive virtue. To understand karma more clearly, let us examine the explanations of karma given in the teachings of **Shakyamuni Buddha.**

According to the sutra teachings of Lord Buddha, there are ten non-virtuous actions and ten virtuous actions that have a direct bearing on karma. Therefore, every complete negative action creates four suffering results, while every complete positive virtuous action creates four happy results. *The ten non virtuous actions* comprise three of the body, four of the speech and three of the mind. Those of the body are killing, stealing and sexual misconduct. Those of speech are telling lies, engaging in slander, harsh speech and gossiping. Those of the mind are covetousness, having ill will towards others and having the wrong views.

190

The ten virtuous actions comprise abstinence of all the non-virtuous actions. Every complete non-virtuous and virtuous action has four suffering and four happy results respectively. And the sum total of these results is the karmic inheritance that defines the type of rebirths that all sentient beings bring with them in their mental continuum. This is karma.

The first of the four results can be described as **the fully ripened result;** where the suffering of negative karma cause rebirths in the suffering lower realms (hell, the realm of hungry ghosts or animal realms). Here one experiences unimaginable sufferings that are far worse than the sufferings of the human realms. The happy result causes rebirths in the body of a happy migratory being in the human or deva realms instead of rebirths in the suffering realms.

The second of the four results is **experiencing a result similar to the cause.** The suffering result is to reborn as human beings and suffer the result of the harmful action committed in the past. If one has killed, one will be killed; and if one has stolen, one will be cheated, if one has slandered others, one will be slandered against... The happy result is rebirth in the human realm with a long and happy life. There will be wealth and enjoyment. And if you have practised the right view you will be reborn with a clear mind, be attracted to virtuous actions, good friends, and right philosophies. You will gravitate to people who help develop your wisdom. You will discover great faith in the Four Noble Truths (True Suffering, True Origin, True Cessation of Suffering, and True Path) and the right view of emptiness. Among the four schools of Buddhist philosophy, you will be especially attracted to the extremely subtle *Prasangika* view, which cuts through the root of samsara, thus eradicating suffering and all its causes. Your strong faith leads you quickly to achieve liberation from samsara. Consequently, you will be able to liberate numberless other sentient beings from all the suffering realms of samsara and bring them to enlightenment with the support of bodhicitta, the pure wish to attain enlightenment for the benefit of all sentient beings.

The third of the four results is **the possessed result.** The suffering result ripens in a future place of rebirth where food is scarce. There is drought, war and famine. The happy result is a glorified place where food, medicines and crops are plentiful. Your rebirth environment is clean, healthy and filled with beauty. The fourth result **creates similar results to the previous cause** ie continuing to commit the same action in the future, and continuing to create the karma over and over again.

All good and bad results of actions can also be experienced in this life. The 10 virtuous actions do not lead only to the happiness of future lives. Most significantly, if the 10 virtuous actions are practised with genuine *bodhicitta,* the altruistic mind to benefit all others, it becomes the cause of the highest ultimate happiness - Enlightenment.

Karma that is repeatedly done becomes very powerful. Karma done in relation to a powerful object such as one's parents, or one's Guru is very powerful. This is as true of the smallest act of disrespect as to the tiniest service or act of love. Karma is definite. It is expandable. Once it is created, good or bad, positive or negative, its results are experienced in many future lifetimes. Sufferings inevitably result from non-virtuous actions for thousands of lifetimes. And negative karma created is irrevocable, unless purified by reading profound sutras, reciting special mantras, or following spiritual practices explained in the holy texts.

Practising genuine compassion toward others, what the Buddhists term the *bodhicitta* mind, can also purify karma. The more compassion one is able to generate toward others, the more one succeeds in achieving powerful purification. Generating compassion has incredible power to purify many eons of negative karma. And it is an especially quick way to collect extensive merit and achieve the peerless happiness of full enlightenment. And if our daily life actions begin with a good heart, then even negative actions can be transformed into virtue.

Even **if you are not Buddhist now**, even if you do not recite Buddhist prayers, if you generate compassion and spend your life serving others, it is the best way of achieving merit. Practising the kind and good heart itself becomes a powerful purification practice; it is also the best cause for your own happiness and success in this life and future lives. Living your daily life with strong compassion, serving others and sacrificing your life for their welfare - this is the way to truly enjoy your life. This is the advice given by the fully enlightened beings. I am offering this advice of Buddha to you. Please take care of your life. I highly recommend this book for people to understand Feng Shui and I ask that people who benefit from Lillian Too's Feng Shui techniques - financial and otherwise can dedicate the merit for the benefit of all sentient beings."

Thank you very much. With love and prayer, "

Lama Zopa
Soquel, California August 1997

The venerable **Lama Thubten Zopa Rinpoche** is the Spiritual Director of the Foundation for the Preservation of the Mahayana Tradition, which comprise ninety-five monasteries and international meditation and healing centers.